THE DOCTRINE OF ULTIMATE REALITY IN SIKH RELIGION

Photograph reproduced with the kind permission of Bibi Gurcharan Kaur, S. Sobha Singh Art Gallery, Andretta (H.P.)

ਗੱਲੀ ਅਸੀ ਚੰਗੀਆ, ਆਚਾਰੀ ਬੁਰੀਆਹ ॥
ਮਨਹੁ ਕੁਸੁਧਾ ਕਾਲੀਆ, ਬਾਹਰਿ ਚਿਟਵੀਆਹ ॥

ਗੁਰੂ ਨਾਨਕ ਦੇਵ

SHREE GURU NANAK DEV

Painting by Sobha Singh

The Doctrine of Ultimate Reality in Sikh Religion

A Study of Gurū Nānak's Hymns in The Ādi Granth

JAMES MASSEY

CENTRE FOR DALIT/SUBALTERN STUDIES

MANOHAR
2010

First published 1991
Reprinted 2010

ISBN 81-85425-38-8

Published by
Ajay Kumar Jain *for*
Manohar Publishers & Distributors
4753/23 Ansari Road, Daryaganj
New Delhi 110 002

Typeset by
Ajay Arts
New Delhi 110002

Printed by
Salasar Imaging Systems
Delhi 110 035

To

Prof. Dr. Edmund Weber
Barbara Weber-Rehberg
in gratitude

and

to

Kala (my wife) and Jyoti, Kiran, Ujwalla (daughters)
for sympathetic endurance

Contents

Preface

In October 1985 I was invited by Prof. Edmund Weber (of the Johann Wolfgang Goethe-University, Frankfurt, West Germany) to give an introductory seminar on Sikhism. I presented a paper on 'A Fresh Look at Sikh Religion' to the members and students of the Faculty of Theology. At the end of the Seminar, Prof. Weber encouraged me to take up a major study on Sikh religion, as part of my doctoral studies. It took me another year to plan this work, before being officially registered for my doctoral study, at the Johann Wolfgang Goethe-University in November 1986. The original title of my work was: 'The Doctrine of the Ultimate Reality in Guru Nanak's Hymns Found in the Standard Text of the Ādi Granth'. This published work contains the complete original study, which was presented to the University, except for editoriai changes in the language.

This work presents a comprehensive study of the cardinal doctrine of the founder Guru of Sikh religion, Nanak. The whole study is divided into five chapters with an introduction in the beginning and a conclusion at the end. Chapter One includes a detailed study of the key phrase of Mūl Mantr, Ik Oṁkār based on the content of Nānak's hymns. Chapter Two presents a brief survey of the names used by Nānak for the Ultimate Reality, in order to grasp a deeper meaning of his cardinal doctrine. In Chapter Three, the various attributes of the Ultimate Reality are studied and in Chapter Four, one of the main attributes, Karatā, the Creator, has been discussed separately. Finally the subject of Chapter Five is Gurparasādi, which is the key to the revelation of the Ultimate Reality. At the end of this work a summary of the whole study is given, followed by a conclusion.

This study would not have been possible without the guidance and help of Prof. Dr. Edmund Weber, and his wife Barbara Weber

Rehberg. Along with Prof. and Mrs. Weber I would like to record my special thanks to Dr. Tilak Raj Chopra of Bonn University for his guidance and to Mrs. Chopra for always accepting me in their home as a family member, during my various visits to Frankfurt and Bonn. I am grateful to the Rt. Revd. Anand Chandu Lal and (the Chairman of the Governing Body of the Indian Society for Promoting Christian Knowledge (ISPCK) and the Bishop of the Diocese of Amritsar, in the Church of North India for his encouragement, particularly for recommending my case for the Martin Niemoeller's Ecumenical Scholarship. I am grateful to the members of the Scholarship Committee, especially to Dr. Paul Loffler for his help in obtaining the required scholarship for this study. There are many friends and well-wishers who encouraged and helped me to complete this work. I am grateful to all of them and to Fr. James Stuart for his editorial assistance in preparing the final manuscript and the members of the Brotherhood of the Ascended Christ for allowing me to use their library freely. Also I am grateful to Fr. Gispert Sauch SJ and the staff of Vidyajyoti Library for all their help. I also thank the ISPCK Executive Committee for their support and my colleague Mr. Ashish Amos and the staff of the ISPCK for taking care of the office work during my study leave. I am particularly grateful to Mrs. Valerie Sadique for typing the manuscript. There are a number of friends in Frankfurt who have been associated with me throughout the period of this study, particularly Rev. Dr. Roger Topelmann and Mr. & Mrs. Meergans of Missionshaus, Bad Homburg for providing me all facilities during my stay in Frankfurt. I am grateful to the Theological Education Desk of the Association of Protestant Churches & Missions (EMW) through Ms. Maureen Trott and Dr. C.O. McMullen of the Christian Institute of Religious Studies, Batala for the financial assistance towards preparing this work for publication as well as for its production. I am indebted to my publisher Mr. Ramesh Jain for his suggestions and keen interest taken by him in this work. Besides these friends, I am thankful to my wife Kala and daughters Jyoti, Kiran and Ujwalla for their constant encouragement. I am grateful to God Almighty for giving me the strength to complete this work.

1 August 1990 JAMES MASSEY
Delhi

Introduction

1. THE SUBJECT AND SCOPE

Among the world religions the Sikh religion is much younger in age, yet its adherents are found all over the world.[1] But in spite of this fact there is hardly any work which deals with the cardinal doctrine of the Sikh religion.[2] It is true that there are some good works[3] which deal with the teachings of Nānak,[4] the founder of the Sikh religion.[5] Also there are works which present the general tenets of Sikh religion.[6] The most notable work in this direction is a recent book

[1]W.H. Mcleod: "The Sikhs of the South Pacific", *Sikh Studies—Comparative Perspectives on a Changing Tradition,* ed. Mark Juergensmeyer and N. Gerald Barrier, Berkeley, 1979, pp. 143-58.

Cole, Owen: "The Sikh Diaspora: Its Possible Effects on Sikhism", *Studies in Sikhism and Comparative Religion,* vol. VII, April-October 1988, pp. 181-96.

S.S. Bhurga: "Sikhs and Sikhism in the United States", *Studies in Sikhism and Comparative Religion,* vol. VI, October 1987, pp. 133-39.

[2] Cf. above, W.H. Mcleod: "A Sikh Theology for Modern Times", *Sikh History and Religion in the Twentieth Century,* ed. Joseph T.O'Connell, Milton Israel, Willard Goxtoby, with visiting eds. W.H. Mcleod, J.S. Grewal, Toronto, 1988, p. 33.

[3] E.g., Mcleod 1968, pp. 148-226.

Anil Chandra Banerjee: *Gurū Nānak and His Times,* Patiala, 1984, pp. 148-77. Gurbachan Singh Talib: *Gurū Nānak—His Personality and Vision,* Delhi, 1969, pp. 107-57.

[4] The spelling of the name 'Nānak' has been used in this work as often used in English. This also applies to other names used in this work.

[5] Mcleod 1975, p. 5.

Trilochan Singh: *Gurū Nānak—Founder of Sikhism* (A Biography), Delhi, 1969, p. XIX.

[6] E.g., Cole, W. Owen and Piara Singh Sambhi: *The Sikhs—Their Religions, Beliefs and Practices,* New Delhi, 1978, pp. 67-103.

Surindar Singh Kohli: *A Critical Study of Ādi Grantha,* Delhi, 1961, pp. 333-68.

Sikh Concept of the Divine edited by Pritam Singh, in which a number of scholars have discussed the various units of the Mūl Mantr, i.e. the basic credal statement of the Sikh religion.[7] But the scope and discussion of this work is limited, because it is mainly confined to the interpretation of the Mūl Mantr.

Therefore the present work takes up the study of the hymns of the founder of the Sikh religion under the title: *The Doctrine of the Ultimate Reality in Sikh Religion: A Study of Gurū Nānak's Hymns, in The Ādi Granth.* The sixth Gurū Hargobind and the tenth Gurū Gobind Singh gave new directions to the Sikh community,[8] but as Mcleod puts it rightly: "The religious content of Sikhism remained, and still remains, the content given by Gurū Nānak."[9] For this reason the present study is limited to the hymns of Nānak.

As is clear from the title of this present work, it does not intend to treat all the aspects of Nānak's theology or his hymns. Its aim is to concentrate on the essentials of Nānak's cardinal doctrine of the Ultimate Reality, which involves dealing with such questions as: Is the Ultimate Reality as seen by Nānak 'absolute' or 'personal' or both? Is it transcendent or immanent or both? How does Nānak address it, or does it have any name? Is this Reality with attributes or without? What is the relationship of this Reality with the visible universe, including human beings? Finally can this Reality be known? If so, how?

2. NĀNAK

The period AD 1400-1650 of Indian history is very important for the historical development of Indian religion, because it was during this period that the most important movement known as the Bhakti Movement reached its climax.[10] This movement was led by a number of poet-saints. Among the most prominent of these are: Rāmānanda (AD 1400-50), Kabīr (AD 1440-1518), Nānak (AD 1469-1539), Mīra Bai (b AD 1449), Sūrdas (16th century), Tulsidas

[7] Pritam Singh, ed.: *Sikh Concept of the Divine*, Amritsar, 1985, pp. 32-127.

[8] Mcleod 1975, pp. 3-4.

[9] Mcleod 1968, p. 3.

[10] D.S. Sarma: *Hinduism Through the Ages*, Calcutta, 1961, pp. 47-57.

(AD 1532-1623), and Tukaram (AD 1598-1649). The common features of the teaching of these poet-saints included: (a) the use of local languages, (b) ignoring caste distinctions, (c) rejecting rituals and ceremonies and (d) laying stress on morality and purity of heart.[11] These poet-saints could be divided into two schools of bhakti, viz. Saguṇa and Nirguṇa. Mīrā Bai and Tulsidas belonged to the first school, who worshipped the Ultimate Reality through the human forms of either Rama or Krishna. Belonging to the second school, the most prominent saints were Kabīr and Nānak, who did not worship the Ultimate Reality in the form of any human being.[12]

Besides the bhakti traditions in general, the other well-known traditions, with which Nānak came into contact, were the Sant and the Muslim Sūfī traditions. The Sant traditions formed part of the Nirguṇa School of Bhakti, which according to Mcleod came into existence because of the Natha influence on the beliefs and practices of Vaisnava bhakti. It is these Sant traditions which have contributed to the thoughts of Nānak.[13] In fact Nānak has been included among the major figures of the northern Sant traditions along with Kabīr and Dadu, because the communities started by these three poet-saints have survived till today. Among these of course the Sikh community is the largest in number and the most important, because it has a very distinct religious way of life and also it grew far larger in size as compared to others.[14]

Besides the above-mentioned important facts about the Sikh Community, Nānak has a special place among the bhakti saints because he was very courageous in dealing with the social evils of

[11] R.C. Majumdar: "Evolution of Religion-Philosophic Culture of India", *The Cultural Heritage of India*, vol. IV, ed. Haridas Bhattacharyya, Calcutta, 1956, p. 60.

[12] See, V. Rahavan: "The Bhakti of Gurū Nānak", *Gurū Nānak—A Homage*, ed. K.R. Srinivasa Iyenger, Sahitya Akademi, New Delhi, 1973, p. 198.

[13] Mcleod, 1975, pp. 6, 7. (For detail discussion see: Mcleod, 1969, pp. 151-63.)

[14] Karine Schomer: "Introduction—The Sant tradition in Perspective", *The Saints—Studies in a Devotional Tradition of India*, ed. Karine Schomer and W.H. Mcleod, Delhi, 1987, p. 6.

his time;[15] his doctrinal thoughts are also very clear, and also his appointing a successor was a unique act, because by doing this he laid the foundation of an ongoing Sikh community/religion.[16]

Whatever is said above about Nānak is true, because all this information can be drawn from the content of his hymns found in the *Ādi Granth*. But there is real difficulty in obtaining historical information regarding Nānak's life. There is no available source, at least from his death in AD 1539 until the middle of the seventeenth century. It seems that information regarding him during these 100 years was passed on orally among his followers, and ultimately took the form of various janam-sākhīs. These sākhīs were put into written form by the middle of the seventeenth century, and contained a mixture of possible historical events of Nānak's life with a number of legends from different sources. Mcleod calls these sākhīs, "hagiographic accounts of the life of Gurū Nānak" and he further adds that these are "more important as description of the seventeenth century Sikh understanding of him than as a contribution to authentic biography."[17] (Among the non-sikh sources about the life of Nānak, references are also found in the writings of the mid-seventeenth century and of the latter part of the eighteenth century.)[18]

But in spite of the above problem with the janam-sākhīs, Mcleod has made an attempt to separate those sākhīs, which are possibly based on legends, from those sākhīs, which can give historical information about the life of Nānak.[19] On the basis of the latter sākhīs, the following possible life sketch can be offered.

[15] See R.C. Majumdar: op. cit., p. 61.

[16] Cf., Mcleod, 1968, p. 150.

[17] Ibid., pp. 8, 9.

[18] *Dabistan-i-Mazahib* in Persian was written (possible author Mohsin Fani) some time during mid-seventeenth century; and a Marathi writing *Bhaktalilamrit* written by Mahipati in AD 1774. Both these writings refer to Nānak.

See, Ganda Singh, ed.: *Sources of the Life and Teachings of Gurū Nānak*, Patiala, 1969, pp. 44-53, 88-9.

[19] Mcleod, 1968, pp. 36-67.

In much detail W.H. Mcleod has dealt the historicity of 'Janam-sākhīs' traditions in his work *Early Sikh Tradition—A Study of the Janam-Sākhīs*, Oxford, 1980. (Particularly see pp. 248-67.)

Nānak was born in AD 1469.[20] His father's name was Kālū and mother's name was Triptā. They belonged to the Khatri caste and lived in a village of Rai Bhoi dī Talvandī (now in Pakistan). Nānak had a sister named Nānakī, who was married to Jai Rām. Nānak's wife was Sulakhanī, whose father Mula lived in Batālā. Nānak had two sons, Lakhmī Dās and Srī Chand.

Nānak worked at Sultānpur. It was here that he had a spiritual vision, which brought about a very radical change in his life. Following this spiritual experience he left his home, travelled very widely and visited many religious places belonging to different religions. This was the time when he deepened and enriched his religious experience, and also began to expound his own views. In the latter part of his life (AD 1522-39), he settled at Kartārpur on the bank of river Rāvī, where he laid the foundation of the Sikh community. Lastly, it was at Kartārpur that he died during September 1539; but before that he had appointed Lahinā, one of his disciples, as his successor to carry on his work and gave him a new name, Angad.

Angad was Gurū from AD 1539 to 1552. After him there were eight other Gurūs: Amar Dās (AD 1552-74), Rām Dās (AD 1574-81), Arjan (AD 1581-1606), Hargobind (AD 1606-44), Har Rai (AD 1644-61), Har Krishan (AD 1661-64), Tegh Bahādur (AD 1664-75) and Gobind Singh (AD 1675-1708). It was the fifth Gurū Arjan under whose direction the compilation of a canonical scripture, i.e. the *Ādi Granth,* took place (AD 1603-4). The tenth Gurū founded the Khālsā in AD 1699. He also added to the *Ādi Granth* the hymns of his father, the ninth Gurū Tegh Bahādur, along with one of his own hymns.

[20] Based upon majority of the sources, the most agreed date of the birth of Nānak is on the third day of the light half of the lunar month of Visakha, Saṁmata 1526, a date which corresponds with 15 April 1469, but traditionally Sikhs continue (even today) to celebrate the birth date during October/November, which is based on the Bālā Janam-sākhīs, i.e. the full moon of Kartaka Saṁmata 1526, which corresponds with 20 October 1469. Cf. Mcleod 1968, p. 94.

Hira Singh Dard, ed.: *Karan Singh Historian Di Itihasak Khoj* (Panjabi), Amritsar, 1975, pp. 3-6.

3. THE *ĀDI GRANTH*

Ādi Srī Gurū Granth Sāhib Jī is the title which is used for the standard published edition of the Sikh scripture. 'Ādi' means 'first' or 'primal', 'Srī' means 'honourable' or 'Lord', 'Gurū' means 'teacher' or 'Lord', 'Granth' means 'book', 'Sāhib' means 'Lord' or 'Master' and 'Jī' is an expression used to show respect. So there are three words with close meanings, i.e. 'Srī', 'Sāhib' and 'Jī', which are used here to show the extraordinary respect for the 'Granth', while the title 'Gurū' indicates its status, because the authority which was previously enjoyed by the personal Gurū, is now entrusted to the 'Granth'.[21] The term 'Ādi' is used to distinguish the first scripture from the other, the *Dasam Granth*, i.e. 'the Book of the tenth Gurū (Gobind Singh)'.[22] There are other shorter titles used for the Sikh scripture, e.g. *Granth Sāhib*, *Gurū Granth Sāhib* and *Ādi Granth*. In the present work the last title *Ādi Granth* has been used in the title as well as throughout the text.

According to well-established tradition the *Ādi Granth* was compiled by the fifth Gurū Arjan during the years 1603-4,[23] but it originated with the hymns of Nānak.[24] The first major collection, in the form of two pothīs, was prepared by Sahansrām, the grandson of the third Gurū Amar Dās, and included the hymns of Nānak, Angad and Amar Dās. These pothīs were kept with Bābā Mohan (the father of Sahansrām), from whom Gurū Arjan took them for

[21] It is a well established tradition among the Sikhs that before the tenth Gurū Gobind Singh died, he commanded them to accept, after him, the *Ādi Granth* as their Gurū.

See, Surinder Singh Kohli: op. cit., p. 19.

[22] *Dasam Granth:* 'Dasam' means 'tenth', and 'Granth' means 'book', which means the 'Book' of the tenth (Gurū)'. The tenth Gurū Gobind Singh wrote many hymns and one of his disciples Bhāī Manī Singh compiled the *Dasam Granth* after 26 years of the death of the tenth Gurū. This 'Granth' is not given the same status as of the *Ādi Granth.*

See C.H. Loehlin: *The Sikhs and Their Scriptures*, Lucknow, 1964, pp. 37-8.

C.H. Loehlin: *The Granth of Gurū Gobind Singh and The Khālsā Brotherhood*, Lucknow, 1971, pp. 10-59.

[23] Cf. Mcleod, 1975 p. 60.

[24] Gurdas: Vāra 1.32.

Vide Cole, W. Owen and Piara Singh, op. cit., p. 18.

use in his own collection.[25] In this Gurū Arjan included the hymns of the first four Gurus, i.e. Nānak, Angad, Amar Dās and Rām Dās, together with his own. He also included the hymns of various saints and bhagatas. The actual copying was done by Bhāī Gurdās under the supervision of Gurū Arjan. This work was completed about the middle of AD 1604. This was the first version of the *Ādi Granth,* which is now with the Soḍhī family[26] of Kartārpur in Jullundur district of Punjāb (in India). This version is also known as Kartārpur Vālī Bīṛ, i.e. the Version of Kartārpur.

So the basic work of the canonization of the *Ādi Granth* was over by AD 1604, but it did not reach its final stage until AD 1705, when the tenth Gurū Gobind Singh added the hymns of his father, the ninth Gurū Tegh Bahādur, along with one of his own hymns. But before that there was one other development which took place, which gave birth to one other version.

When Gurū Arjan's version was completed in AD 1604, one of his disciples became interested in that collection. His name was Bhāī Bānno. He asked Gurū Arjan to be allowed to take the manuscript to his village Māngaṭ. On seeing Bhāī Bānno's interest, Gurū Arjan gave it to him on the condition that he would keep it in his village only for one night. Bhāī Bānno agreed, but took care to complete his journey to his village slowly by walking, and on the way made his own copy of the manuscript. The other tradition ragarding this incident is that Gurū Arjan actually asked Bhāī Bānno to take the original text of the *Ādi Granth* to Lahore for binding, and Bhāī Bānno made his copy while on his way to Lahore.[27]

The problem with Bhāī Bānno's copy of the *Ādi Granth* is that it has extra hymns in it which, it is believed, he retained when copying the original text of Gurū Arjan, although the Gurū had deleted them.[28] These extra hymns are: one hymn of Mīrā Bai, part

[25] Cf., Mcleod, 1975, pp. 60-1.

[26] 'Soḍhī' is the family name of the fifth Gurū Arjan. Therefore after the death of his son the sixth Gurū Hargobind, Soḍhī family inherited the original manuscript of the *Ādi Granth.*

[27] Cf. Mcleod, 1975, p. 75.

[28] Vide, W.H. Mcleod: "The Sikh Scriptures: Some issues", *Sikh Studies—Comparative Perspectives on Changing Traditions,* ed. Mark Juergensmeyer and N. Gerald Barrier, Berkeley, 1979, p. 101.

of a hymn of Surdās, and one hymn of Gurū Arjan, in which he described the mundana ceremony of his son (the sixth Gurū) Hargobind taking place according of the Hindu rite. When the Gurū came to know about Bhāī Bānno's copy, and his retaining in it the deleted hymns, he condemned it as Khārī (literally 'bitter'). Because of this condemnation, this version (bīṛ) has always been considered by the Sikhs as rejected. This was the second version of the *Ādi Granth*, which is now kept in Bhāī Bānno's village Māngaṭ, in the district of Gujarat (now in Pakistan).[29]

The third and final version of the *Ādi Granth* was prepared by Bhāī Manī Singh under the direction of the tenth Gurū Gobind Singh. According to Sikh tradition, this version was dictated by the tenth Gurū from his memory. In this version he added 115 hymns of his father, the ninth Gurū, along with one of his own hymns. This whole work was done at a village known originally as Talvandī Sabo or Sabo Kī Talvandī, but later on it was re-named Damdama (a place of rest), because the tenth Gurū Gobind Singh rested there. This place is in district Bathinda of Punjāb (in India). After the name of this place the third version is known as Damdamī Bīṛ (version) and is considered to be the standard text of the *Ādi Granth*. All the printed copies of the *Ādi Granth* are based on this version and carry this imprint on the title page. The standardization of the pages in number and size took place in the nineteenth century.[30]

In the present work the printed text is based on that of the Damdamī Bīṛ.[31] The point here to be noted is that though the three versions of the *Ādi Granth* mentioned above differ in their contents (i.e. in the case of Bhāī Bānno Vālī Bīṛ, the difference consists in the three hymns of Mīrā Bai, Surdās and Gurū Arjan, and in the case of Damdamī Bīṛ, in the 115 hymns of the ninth Gurū Tegh

[29] Cf., Mcleod, 1975, pp. 74-75.
C.H. Loehlin: "Textual Criticism of the Kartārpur Granth", ed. Mark Juergensmeyer and N. Gerald Barrier, op. cit., p. 117.

[30] Cf. Surinder Singh Kohli: op. cit., pp. 17-19. Mcleod, 1975, p. 75. Cole, W. Owen and Piara Singh Sambhi: op. cit., p. 50.

[31] *Ādi Srī Gurū Granth Sāhib Jī*, Srī Damadamī Bīṛ, Panā 1430, Parkāsak Bhāī Javāhar Singh Kirpāl Singh and Kampanī, Srī Ammritsar. (Access to the original manuscripts are not possible due to political and religious reasons.)

Bahādur and one hymn of the tenth Guru Gobind Singh, added by the latter). where Nānak's hymns are concerned, these remained unchanged in all three versions, and the controversy related to these versions will not affect the present work.

The standard text of the *Ādi Granth* includes a total of 5894 hymns which are attributed to different authors as follows: Nānak 974, Angad 62, Amar Dās 907, Rām Dās 679, Arjan 2218, Tegh Bahadur 115, Gobind Singh 1, and others including bhagatas, 938.[32]

The arrangement of the hymns in the *Ādi Granth* is very systematic. The whole text has three parts.

First: The Introduction (*AG,* pp. 1-13) includes Japu (of Nānak), which is the morning prayer for the Sikhs; So Daru and So Purakhu containing 9 hymns (Nānak 4, Rām Dās 3, Arjan 2), which is part of the evening prayer; and Sohila contains five hymns (Nānak 3, Rām Dās 1, Arjan 1) which is used as the night prayer, as well as at funeral service.

Second: This part forms the main part (*AG,* pp. 14-1353a) of the *Ādi Granth* text. In this part the hymns of Gurus (beginning with Nānak), chronologically followed by Bhagatas' hymns, are arranged under different rāgas. In all there are 31 rāgas used in the *Ādi Granth.* Nānak's hymns are found in the following twenty rāgas: Srī Rāgu, Mājha, Gaurī, Āsā, Gūjarī, Bihāgaṛā, Vadahanu, Sorathi, Dhanāsarī, Tilanga, Sūhī, Bilāvalu, Rāmakalī, Mārū, Tukhārī, Bhairu, Basantu, Sāranga, Malāra and Parbhātī.

Gurūs did not use their personal names (except for the first Gurū, i.e. Nānak), but all adopted 'Nānak' as a common name. In the text their hymns are distinguished by using Mahala 1, 2, 3, 4, 5 and 9, and so there is no problem of identifying the hymns of each Gurū.

Besides the major divisions according to rāgas, there is a further sub-division also found in the text of the *Ādi Granth.* This sub-division is based on the length of stanzas. For example Nānak has used mostly for his hymns caupade (four stanzas) and asatapadia (eight stanzas), etc. The longer works i.e. Nānak's Sidha Gosaṭi, Dakhaṇī Oṁkāru, etc., are placed at the appropriate places according

[32] Cf., Sutantar Singh: *About Srī Gurū Granth Sahib*, New Delhi, 1979, p. 32.

Cole W. Owen, and Piara Singh Sambhi, op. cit., pp. 189-95.

to rāgas. All the hymns of the *Ādi Granth* follow a metrical system.[33]

Third: In this part (*AG*, pp. 1353b-1430) a series of miscellaneous works are found, which include salokas of Nānak, Amar Dās, Rām Dās, Arjan, Tegh Bahādur, Kabīr, Sekha Farīd, etc., and the Savaīe of Arjan and bards.

As mentioned earlier the hymns attributed to Nānak in the *Ādi Granth* total 974. These hymns Nānak wrote at different times during his life.[34] The hymns written during his early years deal with the religious and cultural context in which he was being brought up. Among his early writings is 'paṭṭī' in which he explains the nature of real religious education, which can help one to develop one's faith in the Supreme Lord (parmesaru). The hymns written during his travels deal with more serious issues of life; Dakhaṇī Oṁkāru, Sidha Gosaṭi and Āratī are good examples from this period. One of the main themes of these writings is the Ultimate Reality, to which Nānak addresses in Dakhaṇī Oṁkāru as 'Oṁkāru' (Absolute Being), in Sidh Gosaṭi as 'Param Tanta' (Supreme Reality) and in the Aratī the all-pervading 'Joti' (light). During Nānak's last years at Kartārpur he composed his most important writing, the Japu, in which he deals with the nature of Ultimate Reality and its relationship with all living beings. The other important writing of this period with the same theme is 'Vāra Āsā'.

The Mūl Mantr which is also attributed to Nānak, is his basic theological statement. Not only was it placed by Gurū Arjan at the beginning of the *Ādi Granth*, but also every main section of the *Ādi Granth* opens with it. In the Mūl Mantr, Nānak has given the essence or summary of his doctrine of the Ultimate Reality. Nānak used a unique expression to head the Mūl Mantr—1 Oṁkāru/Ika Oṁkāru—which is repeated 568 times in the *Ādi Granth* as part of the

[33] Vide, Surindar Singh Kohli: op. cit., pp. 66-91.

[34] Lal Singh in his introductory essay to "Hymns of Gurū Nānak" (published by Language Department Punjab, Patiala, 1972, p. 1) has divided Nānak's life in the following three periods: 1. AD 1469-97, 28 years up to receiving the call and spiritual experience; 2. AD 1497-1521, 24 years of extensive travels; 3. AD 1521-39, the time spent with family and congregation till death at Kartārpur.

Cf. Mcleod, 1968, p. 145.

longer and shorter forms of the Mūl Mantr.[35] Nānak, as the author of Mūl Mantr, gave it the most prominent place in order to identify and summarize his thoughts of the Ultimate Reality, and the fifth Gurū Arjan (under whose guidance the *Ādi Granth* was compiled) further confirmed the importance of this expression, along with the complete text of the Mūl Mantr, by placing it at the head of the *Ādi Granth* and every main and sub-section of the same. Accordingly in the present work, this expression has been treated as a key expression and used to initiate the examination of Nānak's hymns. The first chapter of this work begins with it.

4. GENERAL REMARKS

In the present work an attempt is made to understand the views of Nānak by analysing the content of his hymns. This analysis includes the study of the language and phraseology used by Nānak which are derived from different backgrounds. The inner testimony of the hymns is the main basis for capturing the views of Nānak. The references to the various translations and commentaries are intended more to give assistance in this analysis, than to be a study of the historical development of the thoughts of Nānak.

Though the main concern of this study is the hymns of Nānak, yet references have been made to the hymns of other Gurūs including Vārās of Bhāī Gurdās, wherever it is felt that these will help in clarifying the views of Nānak.

There are a number of original technical terms and words in Punjabī used in the text without giving the meanings in the text because this can create a problem in readability. However a glossary of such terms and words is added for convenience at the end.

[35] The Mūl Mantr in five different shorter and longer forms has occurred 568 times in the *Ādi Granth*, which are:

1 Oṁkaru	:	1
1 Oṁkāru sati gura parasādi	:	524
1 Oṁkāru satināmu gura parasādi	:	1
1 Oṁkāru satināmu karatā purakhu gura parasādi	:	9
1 Oṁkāru satināmu karatā purakhu nirabhaū niravairu akāla mūrati ajūnīsaibhaṁ gura parasādi	:	33
		568

In all the five forms Ik Oṁkāru has occurred every time.

Cf. Jagjit Singh Saluja: *Mūl mantr*, Ludhiana, 1982, pp. 2, 11.

For transcribing Gurmukhi spellings, the system used by C. Shackle for his work *A Gurū Nānak Glossary*[36] has been used in this study except the proper names. The terminology used by Nānak is quoted in its original Punjābī form in the present work. It is derived from Sanskrit, but is not identical with the original Sanskrit forms.

[36] Shackle: pp. XIX-XXIII.

Prologue

MŪL MANTR

1(the figure)[1] Oṁkār[2] sati nāmu karatā purakhu nirabhau niravairū akāla mūrati ajūnī saibhaṁ[3] gura parasādi[4]

THE BASIC CREDAL STATEMENT

(There is) one Absolute Being with true identity; (who is) Creator Being, without fear, without hostility, eternal Being, free from the limitation of human birth, self-born (and is known) by the favour of Gurū.

[1] As the first letter of Mūl Mantr is given in the figure '1' in the original text, thereof it is given here also in figure not in word.
[2] According to early Sikh tradition the pronunciation of the second word of Mūl Mantr is Oṁkār, as printed here (see Gurdās, 3:15 and ch. 1, n. 1). Nānak has also used the full form Oṁkāru in one of his important works, the Dakhaṇī Oṁkār, as 'Oṁkār' (see *AG*, 929).
[3] On the basis of the spelling given in the Mūl Mantr it is transcribed as 'saibhaṁ', but this word, when spoken, commonly has a nasal sound after the diphthong 'ai' and already above the consonant 'bh' there is nasal sign anusvāra.
[4] Here the letters of Mūl Mantr have been written separately for convenience sake, but in the original text, including the standard printed text, these words are written together, without being separated.

CHAPTER ONE

Ik Oṁkār

1.1. INTRODUCTION

The phrase Ik Oṁkār[1] has a unique place in the Sikh religion. It heads the basic credal statement, the Mūl Mantr of the Sikh religion, or the religion of Nānak, its founder. Parma Nand has rightly said: ". . . the mūl mantr is the gist of the whole sacred bani and contains in a nutshell seeds of all the principles of the Sikh religion. . . . The phrase 'Ek Oṁkār' is the absolute essence of the whole mūl mantra."[2] Because of this unique position, it is important to begin the study of the most cardinal doctrine of Nānak (i.e. the Ultimate Reality) with an examination of the phrase which he himself chose to head his basic theological statement.

1.2. INTERPRETATION OF IK OṀKĀR

Nānak never used Ik Oṁkār in his hymns as a compound phrase as it is used in the Mūl Mantr. At the same time Mūl Mantr is a very concentrated statement, which can only be interpreted; it is

[1] In the original text of the *Ādi Granth* Ik Oṁkāru is written as ੴ. The first letter here is fugure One, i.e. '1' and the second letter is actually a combination of two parts, i.e. first Gurmukhi letter 'Uṛā' and the other on the top with an extended symbol '⌒'. According to Sikh tradition the figure '1' is written in words as 'Ik' or 'Ek' (both these spellings are common in Punjābī, but in this present study the first spelling 'Ik', is used) 'Uṛā' is written as 'Oṁ' and the symbol '⌒' as 'Kāru'. The full phrase is written as Ik Oṁkāru.

Cf. Gurdās 3.15, Vir Singh 1981, pp. 4-6, Sāhib Singh, p. 44.

[2] Parma Nand: 'Ek Oṁkār', *Sikh Concept of the Divine*, ed. Pritam Singh, Amritsar, 1985, p. 55.

Also Cf., Jagjit Singh Saluja: *Mūl Mantr* (Punjābī), Ludhiana, pp. 1-2, 39.

practically impossible to translate it. For this reason, most of the available translations of the Mūl Mantr differ in their renderings (see 1.2.1). What the translators offer are only paraphrases, which are influenced either by personal beliefs or by already existing religious traditions. This is particularly true of the translations and interpretations of Ik Oṁkār, which is the first and the key phrase of the Mūl Mantr. Therefore in order to find what may be the correct meaning/interpretation of Ik Oṁkār an attempt is here made first, to make a brief survey of the major translations and commentaries available in various languages, mainly in English and Punjābī, and then to examine the content of Nānak's hymns (see 1.3.). The major translations and commentaries help us to see the problem relating to the meaning of Ik Oṁkār, and the examination of the content of Nānak's hymns helps us to understand the meaning of Ik Oṁkār and also the content of his cardinal doctrine.

1.2.1. TRANSLATIONS

There are only three translations available in English of the complete text of the *Ādi Granth*, which have been done by Gopal Singh (1960), Man Mohan Singh (1962) and Gurbachan Singh Talib (1984). The earliest translations of the partial text of the *Ādi Granth* were those of Ernest Trumpp (1877) and Max Arthur Macauliffe (1909).

Then there are some well-known English translations of Japu which include the translation of Mūl Mantr also. These include: Teja Singh (1919), Sohan Singh (1958), Puran Singh (1969), Dewan Singh (1970), and W.H. Mcleod (1984). The most recent translation of Japu is in German by Monika Thiel-Horstmann (1988).

The above translators rendered Ik Oṁkār in the following way:

Ernest Trumpp: "Om"[3]
Macauliffe: "There is but one God"[4]
Gopal Singh: ". . . The One Supreme Being. . ."[5]

[3] Trumpp: p. 1.
[4] Macauliffe: vol. 1, p. 195.
[5] Gopal Singh: vol. 1, p. 1.

Man Mohan Singh: "There is but on God"[6]
Talib: "He is the Sole Supreme Being"[7]
Teja Singh: ". . . the One Supreme Being"[8]
Sohan Singh: "The One Universal Being"[9]
Puran Singh: "He is One. He is the First. He is all that is."[10]
Dewan Singh: "God is One and all-pervading".[11]
W.H. Mcleod: "There is one Supreme Being"[12]
Monika Thiel-Horstmann: "Ein Gott",[13] i.e. "One God".

All these translators on the basis of their above renderings can be divided into four groups: (i) Ernest Trumpp; (ii) Macauliffe, Man Mohan Singh, Dewan Singh and Thiel-Horstmann; (iii) Gopal Singh, Talib, Teja Singh and Mcleod; (iv) Sohan Singh, Puran Singh and Dewan Singh.

The translators belonging to groups (ii) and (iii) render Oṁkāru as "God) or "Supreme Being". The fourth group render Oṁkāru as "Universal Being", "He is all that is" and "all-pervading". None of these translators, including Trumpp, have given any explanation of how they arrived at their rendering, except Gopal Singh, who according to his own explanation given in the footnote, seems to have been influenced by the views of Swami Vivekananda and Kapur Singh. According to Swami Vivekananda, Oṁkāru is: "A symbolic word meaning the Supreme Being", and Kapur Singh says about the figure '1' that it 'does not merely signify God's unity . . . , but also affirms His Being a personality. . . .'[14] Even these two views, along with the various renderings quoted above, only

[6] Man Mohan Singh: vol. 1, p. 1.
[7] Talib: vol. 1, p. 1.
[8] Teja Singh, Trans.: *Japji*, Amritsar, 7th edn., 1974, p. 19.
[9] Sohan Singh: *The Seeker's Path* (*Being an Interpretation of Gurū Nānak's Japuji*), Bombay, 1959, p. 1.
[10] Puran Singh, Trans: *Japuji Sahib*, Amritsar, p. 64.
[11] Dewan Singh: *Gurū Nānak's Message in Japuji*, Amritsar, 1970, p. 81.
[12] Mcleod 1984, p. 86.
(The whole text of Japuji's translation is found on pp. 86-93.)
[13] Monika Thiel-Horstmann: *Lehen Aus Der Wahrheit* (in German), Benziger, 1988, p. 35.
[14] Gopal Singh: vol. 1, p. 1 (fn.).

indicate the complicated nature of the problem connected with the meaning and the understanding of Ik Oṁkār. Therefore the only way to reach some reasonable understanding of this key expression is to examine Nānak's own hymns; but before that a few selected Punjābī language commentators' views will be worth looking at also.

1.2.2. Commentaries

Not many commentaries have been written on the text of the *Ādi Granth*. There are only three main attempts in Punjābī, out of which only two are complete:

i. *Ādi Srī Gurū Granth Sāhib Jī-Sātīka* (Farīdakot Vālā Tīkā in 4 vols.), 1899.
ii. *Srī Gurū Granth Darapaṇ* by Sāhib Singh (10 vols.), 1961.
iii. *Santhyā Srī Gurū Granth Sāhib* by Bhāī Vīr Singh (7 vols. as far as Rāga Āsā).

The first commentary known as Farīdakot Vālā Tīkā was done by Gyānī Badan Singh with the assistance of a group of scholars. This tīkā was a response to Trumpp's translation of the *Ādi Granth*, with which Sikhs were not happy. So in 1877 when Trumpp's translation appeared, Gyānī Badan Singh, along with other scholars, was requested by the Sikh ruler of Farīdakot to undertake this work in order to produce a correct tīkā on the *Ādi Granth*. Work on the tīkā was started in 1877 and was completed in 1883. It was published in 1899. The second commentary, the *Srī Gurū Granth Sāhib Darapaṇ*, was the work of a single man, Sāhib Singh, who started this work in 1920, and completed it in 1961. The third attempt was that of Bhāī Vīr Singh, who could only complete his tīkā as far as *Rāga Āsā*, when he died in 1957.

There are many tīkās available of some part of the *Ādi Granth*, particularly of Japu, and some of these will be referred to in this section along with the above three main tīkās. But we will begin our examination with the Vārs of Bhāī Gurdās (1546-1637), which are considered to be 'key' to the *Ādi Granth*.[15]

[15] Cf. Mcleod, 1968, p. 14.

1.2.2.1. *Bhāī Gurdās*

Bhāī Gurdās is the earliest commentator, and his views are most important, because he lived during the lifetime of four Sikh Gurūs, Amar Dās (AD 1552-74), Rām Dās (AD 1574-81), Arjan (AD 1581-1606) and Har Gobind (AD 1606-45). His writings must have been known to these Gurūs, He is also the man who helped Gurū Arjan in the compilation of the *Ādi Granth.*[16] All this adds importance to his views. Gurdās in his Vār 3: 15 while giving a commentary on the Mūl Mantr says about Ik Oṁkār:

Ekā ekaṁkāru likhi dekhāliā
üṛā Oṁkār pāsi bahāilia[17]

He affirmed by writing unique One (the figure 1)
(which is) ekaṁkār (unique), and placed it near üṛā (O)
(which is) Oṁkār.

According to Gurdās, the figure '1' here represents ekaṁkāru and gurmukhī üṛā represents Oṁkār. Gurdās also gives the meaning of ekaṁkāru and Oṁkār in a number of places in his Vārs.[18] For example he says in Vār 26.2:

Niraṁkāru ākāru hoi ekaṁkāru apāru sadāiā
ekaṁkāru sabada dhunī oṁkāri ākāru baṇāiā[19]

After taking form,
the Formless became One.
From One originates the syllable-sound,
which has the form of Oṁkār.

Gurdās in this verse described the process by which Niraṁkāru, i.e. the formless (One), through different stages took form. The process according to him is:

Niraṁkāru → (ākāru) → ekaṁkāru → (sabada dhunī) Oṁkār

[16] See Introd., p. 10.
[17] Gurdās: 3.15.
[18] Gurdās: 1.4; 4.1; 6.4; 13.11; 18.7, 11; 19.11; 22.1; 26, 5, 35; 37, 1, 2; 39.2, 4, 13, etc.
[19] Gurdās: 39.2.

Niraṁkāru, the 'Formless', by taking form (ākāru) became ekaṁkāru, and then from ekaṁkāru became the sabada dhunī (syllable-sound), which is the next stage of the Niraṁkāru which Gurdās calls Oṁkāru. By ekaṁkāru Gurdās means ikāṁga, i.e. 'One',[20] and by Oṁkār he means dhunī, i.e. 'syllable-sound'.[21] So here is the process by which the 'Formless' first took the form of 'One' and then became syllable Sound':

The Formless → (form) → One syllable → (sabad dhunī) Oṁkār.

This discussion of Gurdās makes clear what he understood from Ik Oṁkār, i.e. 'One Word Sound' (ikāṁga sabad dhunī) of the Formless (Niraṁkāru). Gurdās in his Vār 26:35 also adds with dhunī another word, anahadu, which literally means 'unstruck' but as this word anahadu refers to that final experience of a yogi or mystic, which he experiences at the climax of his yoga or mystical devotion;[22] it, therefore, adds a special meaning to dhnuī or sound. so the full meaning of Ik Oṁkār according to Gurdās is 'One mysterious Word Sound'.

Gurdās of course did not restrict his discussion only to the meaning of Ik Oṁkār; he also goes further and says that the Formless who took the form of 'One Word (or mysterious) Sound', is also behind everything that we see in the universe. Oṁkār according to him is the agent of creation of all things, so Niraṁkāru became Karatāru (Creator) also. Because he is Karatāru, he is, therefore, also paravadagāru, the provider of all the needs of creation.[23]

1.2.2.2. *Gyānī Badan Singh*

The purpose of his commentary, known as the Farīdakota vālā Tīkā, was to present a correct interpretation of the *Ādi Granth* as a response to Ernest Trumpp's work.[24] The whole Tīkā is a kind of paraphrase of the *Ādi Granth*, through which an attempt has been made to give the meaning of the text.

[20] Gurdās: 39.1.

[21] Gurdās: 26.1.

[22] Shackle: S.V., anahadu, p. 16.

[23] Gurdās: 21.1.

[24] Farīdakota: vol. 1, Introd., p. 'ūṛā'.

Gyānī Badan Singh in interpreting the Mūl Mantr, particularly Ik Oṁkār, made his doctrinal position clear from the start. While commenting on the figure '1', he says "Jo Sidhānta Vastu advaita hai dvaita nahim"[25] means "that doctrinal reality which is non-dual, not dual." He also says in the next clause that jīv (living being) and 'Isa' are 'eka rūpa' (of one form or non-different).

Gyānī Badan Singh stressed that the figure '1' is a veil before Oṁkār, so that persons belonging to a low caste and women may also use it in their devotion, because otherwise these two groups were not allowed to repeat the syllable Oṁ.

Basically Gyānī Badan Singh accepts the Vedantic position in his interpretation, because he does not see living beings as the creation of a creator. According to him:

> *Ekarai kā arthu ādutī niraguṇa paramātmā hai*
> *Vahī apani māiā saktī sāth milkar akāra ukāra makāra tīna rūpa hūā.*[26]

> The meaning of figure '1' is the unique attributeless the Supreme Soul (Paramātmā), who through his illusory power took the form of akāra, ukāra and makāra, i.e. a, u and m together forming 'om'.

For Gyānī Badan Singh Mūl Mantr began with Oṁkār, and he takes it literally as Oṁ. He further divides the syllable Om into three parts, i.e. 'a', 'u' and 'm' which he considered as three roots—akāra from 'a', ukāra from 'u', and makāra from 'm'. Further his explanation of these parts of Oṁ is based on the Indian religious tradition: akāra according to him means Virat Iśvara or Universal Being, the awakened state of the Lord, of Being; ukāra means hiranya (light) garbha Iśvara, Taijas Jīva (Glorious Being), the dream state; makāra means Iśvara, who is the Lord of Māiā (illusion), the state of deep sleep.[27]

This summary of Gyānī Badan Singh's views makes the following points clear about Ik Oṁkār:

> First, he has understood the figure '1' in its functional aspect, i.e. as a veil.

[25] Ibid., see p. 1, top.
[26] Ibid., p. 2.
[27] Ibid., see p. 1, below.

Second, it is clear, that for him Ik Oṁkār is simply 'Om',

1.2.2.3. *Sāhib Singh*

Sāhib Singh has used a very simple method to interpret Ik Oṁkār. He divided it into three parts—Ik, Oṁ, Kar. Then he states the three uses of Oṁ:

- i. Use of Oṁ as a sacred syllable in the beginning and ending of Vedas, other religious books, prayers or any other works.
- ii. Use of Oṁ as answer while answering any order or question, as a mark of respect.
- iii. Oṁ as Brahman.

Sāhib Singh says that any of the above meanings can be taken and then the figure '1' is added before it, in order to put the stress on that meaning. However, he concludes that the meaning of Oṁ is: "One Being, who is incomparable and in whom this whole universe is contained."[28] 'Kār' according to Sāhib Singh, is a Sanskrit suffix, which is normally used with nouns. It means 'One unchangeable essence'. Sāhib Singh has taken the figure '1' as ekaṁkāru with the meaning 'One'. He concludes his discussion: Therefore the pronunciation of the figure '1' along with ūṛā' is Ik Oṁkāru and it means One timeless Being (Akāla Purakha), who is all-pervading in one essence.[29]

1.2.2.4. *Bhāī Vīr Singh*

Bhāī Vīr Singh has not only given his own meaning of Ik Oṁkār in the beginning of his tīkā on Japu, which is a part of the first volume of *Santhyā Srī Gurū Granth Sāhib,* but has also discussed in detail all the aspects of Ik Oṁkār, drawing support from the *Ādi Granth,* Vārs of Gurdās and other Indian religious literature. Here we refer only to his main conclusion. Bhāī Vīr Singh also begins his analysis by accepting the three basic parts of Ik Oṁkār, i.e. Ik, Oṁ and Kār. About the figure '1' or Ik he says: "The meaning of the figure '1' is: There is only one principal being, which never changes, which never became a second."[30] The figure '1' was added

[28] Sāhib Singh, p. 44.
[29] Ibid., p. 46.
[30] Vir Singh, 1981, p. 11.

by Nānak, according to Bhāī Vir Singh, to show the disassociated aspect of the Formless.[31] According to him the 'Formless' (Niraṁkār), who is unique in nature, lives in every heart, and to communicate this thought Nānak placed the figure '1' before Oṁkār.[32] He also adds that Oṁkār is 'spirit', that it cannot be measured and there is nothing which can be called its second. He of course has rejected the traditional interpretation of Oṁkār, according to which the three matras of Oṁ represent: A Shiva, O Vishnu and U Brahman. He says the figure '1' indicates that Oṁkāru cannot be divided.[33] The meaning of Kār according to Bhāī Vīr Singh is 'only'. Therefore the meaning of Oṁkār is 'Only Oṁ'.[34] On the basis of the above discussion Bhāī Vīr Singh's understanding of Ik Oṁkār can be stated as: There is only One Primal Being (mūla hasti).

1.2.2.5. *Other Tīkās*

There are two important tīkās on Japu, which call for notice, the first by Vinoba Bhave in Hindi and the second by Bhāī Jodh Singh. Bhave's comment on Ik Oṁkār is worth noting:

> In the beginning is written the figure '1' not the word 'one'. The basis of all religion is the Unity of God. Oṁkār is a sound-symbol as well as a syllable. This kind of word helps in meditation. Oṁkār is accepted as the essence of Vedic knowledge. Both Upanishad and Gita have used this word. By using the same word Gurū Nānak has maintained that tradition . . . when a new idea based on the old one takes birth, then it has a new flavour as well as the strength of the old.[35]

Bhāī Jodh Singh begins his discussion on Ik Oṁkār by referring to various interpretations of it which are based on different roots of Oṁ found in Sanskrit. But he concludes by saying: "Whatever the root of Oṁ may be, without any doubt it can be said that this phrase signifies Brahman."[36] But he continues his argument by pointing

[31] Ibid., p. 4.
[32] Ibid., p. 5.
[33] Ibid., p. 10.
[34] Ibid., p. 6.
[35] Vinoba: *Japuji* (Mūla ke Sāth), Varanasi, 3rd edn., 1965, p. 33.
[36] Bhāī Jodh Singh: *Japuji Satīka*, Patiala, 1980, p. 1.

out that because some people started dividing Oṁ into three parts representing three gods or three states, therefore Nānak placed the figure '1' before Oṁ and added 'Kar' as a suffix, and in this way he made it only a symbol of Brahman. Therefore finally Bhāī Jodh Singh concludes: "There is only 'One', who is signified by this syllable Oṁ." He also adds that Ik Oṁkār "represents that indescribable state of the Formless, which he had before becoming Creator."[37]

1.3. NĀNAK HIMSELF ON IK OṀKĀR

In this section Nānak's own views on Ik Oṁkār as found in his hymns are examined. This section has been divided under the following sub-themes. These are selected on the basis of some prominent expressions used by Nānak in his hymns:

i. a. Ik, Ekaṁkāru etc.
   b. Avaru Nā Dūja
   c. Eka Mahi Saraba Saraba Mahi Eka
   d. Nirālā
ii. Oṁkār
iii. Ik Oṁkār

1.3.1. Ik, Ekaṁkāru, etc.

i. *Sāhib merā eko hai*
eko hai bhāī eko hai.[38]

My Lord is One,
He is One, He is One, brother.

ii. *Ekama ekaṁkāru nirālā*
Amaru ajonī jāti na jālā
Agama agocaru rūpu na rekhā.
Khojata Khojata ghati ghati dekhiā.[39]

On the first day,
One Absolute Being—unique, eternal,
unincarnated, without identity,

[37] Ibid., p. 2.
[38] *AG*, p. 350.
[39] *AG*, p. 838.

without impurity, inaccessible, imperceptible, without form
or outline;
but through an ongoing search,
(I have) seen (Him) in each and every heart.

In the first hymn Nānak, using very simple words, but very forcefully, introduces the idea of 'One' or 'oneness' of his 'Lord' or 'Master'. Three times he uses the same word 'eko' which means 'One'. This form 'eko' ending with 'o' shows the stress Nānak would like to put on it. The ending 'o' does not leave any possibility of there being a second or other. The simple word 'eka' can have a number of possible renderings, e.g. one, single, alone, only, firm, unchanged, single of its kind, unique, singular, chief, supreme, prominent sole, etc.[40] But it seems that by the repeated use of 'eko' with 'hai' (meaning 'is') Nānak has attempted to convey all the above meanings of 'eka'. In poetical form the statement has become far more forceful. The expression used here looks somewhat liturgical in nature. The above-quoted stanza is part of the opening verse of a longer hymn. This opening verse ends with an instruction 'vahau', meaning 'pause', and during this 'pause' listeners are supposed to meditate on the point stated before.[41] This 'pause' is also used as indicating the introduction of an important subject. And here the subject on which the listeners are to meditate is 'eko', i.e. the One Lord of Nānak. He has used here a personal title 'Sāhib', which points out that the 'One' whom he is addressing is not an abstract idea: but He is one who by nature is 'One', or even 'absolute; and yet one with whom one can enter into personal relationship. He brings out the idea of the 'one' still more powerfully in the second hymn quoted above.

In the second hymn, Nānak has stated the absolute nature of his 'One' as well as his all-pervading nature. One of the concerns of Nānak's hymns is to communicate the 'Oneness' (possibly rightly, the—'absoluteness') of the Ultimate Relaity, for which in this hymn he uses the strongest possible title, 'ekaṁkāru'. This title is perhaps the one unique expression, which Nānak himself coined to express

[40] S.V., Apte: eka, p. 311.
Monier-Williams: eka, p. 227.

[41] See Kahan Singh, p. 1014.

his thought about the Ultimate Reality, and is clearly the combination of two words, ekaṁ and kāru. Ekaṁ ordinarily means 'one' and refers to 'number', but here it has been used as a masculine noun, which means the 'One'.[42] Further the suffix 'karu' is added which means 'only'[43] from which the absolute nature of the 'One' or the One Reality becomes clear.

In another hymn Nānak states the same point more clearly, when he says:

Ekaṁkāru avaru nā dūjā Nānak eku samāī.[44]

(There is only) One Absolute Being. No one else at all (besides Him); Nānak is always merged (in Him) Who is only One.

Nānak does not simply declare the new title of his Lord, he goes on to justify the same truth or to give the explanation, why his Lord is absolute in nature. It is because he is unique, eternal, unincarnated, without identity, without impurity, inaccessible, imperceptible and without any form or outline. All these qualities or attributes of Nānak's Lord separate him from the ordinary living beings or things of this universe. Through these attributes Nānak brings out the transcendental aspect of his Lord. In the same way in one other hymn Nānak describes him as the Supreme Reality, and repeatedly uses the following expression to express this aspect:

Parama tanta mahi rekha na rūpu.[45]

The Supreme Reality has no outline or form.

Apart from the above hymns, in a number of other hymns Nānak uses many other phrases and expressions to communicate the concept of the 'One' and its absolute nature, for example,

Iku dātā (One Giver),[46] Iku dhatu (One Essence),[47] jugu jugu eku ves (ages to ages One Form),[48] sācā sāhibu eku (True Lord

[42] Cf., Shackle, p. 29.
[43] See Vir Singh, 1981, p. 6.
[44] *AG.*, p. 930.
[45] *AG*, pp. 952-3.
[46] *AG*, p. 2.
[47] *AG*, p. 5.
[48] *AG*, p. 7.

One),[49] sadā sadā tuṁ eku (you are always, yes always One),[50] hari ikaṁkāru (One Absolute Lord),[51] eku nirañjanu (One Pure Being),[52] Parbhū eku (One Lord),[53] Gurū eko (One Teacher),[54] Karatā tu eko (you One Creator),[55] eka murāri (One Murāri),[56] eko bhavaru (One Soul),[57] eko pātisāhu (One King),[58] etc.

Nānak not only recognises the One Absolute Reality/Being, but he also experiences its presence everywhere, especially in every human being. This is what he means by the expression: ghati ghati dekhiā (seen in each and every heart). Here the immanent aspect of the nature of One Absolute Reality/Being is expressed.

1.3.2. Avaru Nā Dūjā

To lay further stress on the concept of the 'One' as well as on Its uniqueness Nānak repeatedly uses the expression, avaru nā dūjā (no one else at all). Reference has already been made to one of Nānak's important hymns, Dakhanī Oaṁkāru, which reads: ekaṁkāru avaru nā dūjā Nānak . . . (there is only One Absolute Being, no one else at all besides Him . . .). [59] Besides this there are many other hymns of Nānak which state the same idea. Some examples are:

i. *Nānak eko ravi rahiā dūjā avaru nā koi.*[60]

   Nānak only One lives (everywhere).
   certainly there is no second one there.

ii. *Asati eka digari kuī.*
   Eka tuī eka tuī.[61]

   Only One is (there),

[49] *AG*, p. 15.
[50] *AG*, p. 139.
[51] *AG*, p. 222.
[52] *AG*, p. 223.
[53] *AG*, p. 355.
[54] *AG*, p. 358.
[55] *AG*, p. 903.
[56] *AG*, p. 908.
[57] *AG*, p. 930.
[58] *AG*, p. 1188.
[59] See Sec. 1.3.1. (reference no. 44).
[60] *AG*, p. 57.
[61] *AG*, p. 144.

There is no one else
You alone, (yes) you alone (are there).

iii. *Eko levai eko devai avaru nā dūjā mai suniā.*[62]

One takes One gives, about no one else I have heard.

iv. *Avaru nā dīsai kisu sālāhī tisah sariku nā koi.*[63]

No one else is seen,
whom should I praise,
no one else is there to equal Him.

v. *Jo antari so bāhari*
dekhahu avaru nā dūjā koi jīu.[64]

He is inside, see Him Outdie also,
Without Him no one else is there.

vi. *Tribhavana joti dharī Paramesari avaru nā dūjā bhāīye.*[65]

The light of the Supreme Lord fills the three worlds,
No one else except him is there, O brother.

All the above six stanzas quoted from different hymns of Nānak have this in common, that the content of all these is the outcome of his own personal experience. In the first hymn, Nānak affirms the certainty of his faith in the existence of the 'One'. There is not the slighest suggestion that there could be a 'second' besides the 'One'. Nānak puts the same idea more emphatically in the second hymn, which is in Persian,[66] 'Eka tuī eka tuī (you alone, you alone). In the repeated phrase 'eka tuī', the term 'tuī' is the emphatic form of 'tuṁ' (you), through which Nānak directly addresses his 'One' (Ultimate Being). His 'One' is the one who controls the destiny of all. In the third hymn Nānak expresses this idea through expressions: 'eko levai' (One takes) and 'eko devai' (one gives).

The fourth hymn, in which Nānak has used Arabic phrases, again shows how his hymns are based on his personal experience. He sees only 'One Reality', worthy of praise, to which nothing else can be equal. Nānak has used a very common term 'sarīku' to convey this

[62] *AG*, p. 433.
[63] *AG*, p. 597.
[64] *AG*, p. 599.
[65] *AG*, p. 1024.
[66] S.V., 'tuī'. Shackle, p. 143.

concept of the 'One' or 'Absolute'. In modern Panjābī 'sarīk' is commonly used in the singuler form 'sarīka' to refer to neighbours (particularly in a village situation), whose relationship is one of equality because they belong to the same ethnic group. Here Nānak refers to the fact that there is no other 'reality' or 'realities' (god or gods), because his experience tells him there is only the One, which he has seen everywhere (antari-bāhari, inside-outside). In the last hymn Nānak uses the title Paramesari (the supreme Lord) for the One Absolute Reality, which again he sees as all-pervading through His light (jotī). Here again an important point to be noted is that Nānak continually uses the personal title 'Sāhibu' (Lord) for his 'One'.[67]

1.3.3. Eka Mahi Saraba Saraba Mahi Eka

Eka mahi saraba saraba mahi eka satigura dekhi dikhāī.
Jini kīe khanda mandala brahamanḍā So parbhu lakhanu na jāī.
Dīpaka te dīpaka paragāsiā tribhavaṇa jotī dikhāī.[68]

All in One, One in all,
This vision was shown (to me) by the true Gurū.
The one who made continents, orbits and universe, that Lord can not be seen.
From One Lamp was lit (another) lamp, in this way he has shown (the pervading) Light of the three worlds.

The above three stanzas are part of a hymn found in the Rāmakali rāga. This hymn deals with the role of the Gurū. The Gurū is here seen as a guide leading a disciple to the vision of the 'One', whom Nānak addresses as 'Lord', who is the Creator of this World, though He is unknown. This latter point is the theme of the second stanza quoted above. In the third stanza the way in which this unknown Creator Lord can be known, is expressed as 'Dīpaka te dīpaka paragāsiā' (from One Lamp was lit another lamp). This means that the true Gurū who is himself the Lamp which is already alight, helps others to see the Light (joti), which pervades the three worlds. This explanation of the third stanza can help in understanding what Nānak means by the phrases 'eka mahi saraba' (all in One) or 'saraba

[67] *AG*, pp. 421, 689, etc.
[68] *AG*, p. 907.

mahi eka' (One in all). Here the stress is on the all-pervading presence or immanent nature of the One Creator Lord. Unless we take into consideration the content of the whole hymn or the immediately succeeding stanzas, the literal meaning of these phrases can mislead us in the understanding of Nānak's concept of 'Oneness'. There are a number of other hymns in which he speaks still more clearly about the immanent nature of the 'One' e.g.

i. *ākāsi pātāli tuṁ tribhavaṇi rahiā samāī,*[69]

You continue to pervade the firmanent, the nether region and the three worlds.

ii. *eko nāmu eku Nārāiṇu tribhavaṇa ekā jotī.*[70]

(There is) One Name, One Lord,
and One Light in the three worlds.

iii. *Tribhavaṇa joti dharī paramesri avaru nā dūjā bhāīre.*[71]

The Supreme Lord's Light pervades the three worlds.
There is no one else, O brother!

In the three hymns quoted above two points are common: first, the 'Oneness' of the Lord, whom Nānak addresses as Nārāiṇu and paramesri; and second, that He lives everywhere and pervades the entire cosmos (tribhavaṇu, i.e. the three worlds). None of these hymns suggest the tribhavaṇu is the same as the 'One' or 'the Creator Lord'.

There is one other expression used by Nānak which needs attention here: sohaṁ haṁsa (he is I and I am He).[72] Nānak has also used this expression in one of his salokas in rāga Māru, from which the following stanza is quoted:

Nānak sohaṁ hamsā japu jāpahu tribhavaṇa tisai samahi.[73]
Nānak repeats this prayer:
He is I and I am He.
The three worlds are pervaded by Him.

This hymn, particularly the expression 'sohaṁ hamsā', very clearly

[69] *AG*, p. 62.
[70] *AG*, p. 992.
[71] *AG*, p. 1024.
[72] S.V. Sohaṁ in Shackle, p. 57.
[73] *AG*. p. 1093.

indicates that the human 'self' and the 'One' or the 'Creator Lord' are non-different. The same is once again said about tribhavaṇa and 'Him', but the relationship of tribhavaṇa with the 'One' was explained above while discussing the earlier hymn. Here the concern is with what Nānak really means by the expression 'sohaṁ haṁsā'. Again its meaning can be understood by looking at some of the hymns, where Nānak has dealt more particularly with the relationship of the human 'self' with the One Ultimate Being or the 'One'. Some examples from these hymns are:

i. *Ghati ghati ravi rahiā alakha arāre Rām*[74]

   Invisible and infinite Ram remains dwelling in every heart.

ii. *Antari sunnu bāhari sunna tribhavaṇa sunam sunna.*[75]

   Within (us) Absolute, outside (us) Absolute, and Absolute in the three worlds.

iii. *Gupata pargata hari ghati ghati dekhahu varatai tāku sabāiā*[76]

   I see (you) Hari as unmanifested as well as manifested in every heart.
   The Unique (Lord) pervades all.

These three hymns teach one common point, namely, the continual presence of the Absolute Lord in the human heart. A possible implication and meaning of the expression 'sohaṁ haṁsa' can be found in the light of these hymns. If so, then Nānak's concept of all pervasiveness of 'One' can be understood better. This truth Nānak has repeatedly stated in a number of other hymns besides the ones quoted above.[77]

From the discussion in this sub-section, one thing becomes clear, that Nānak has sometimes used difficult expressions like 'eka mahi saraba saraba mahi eka' and 'sohaṁ haṁsā', which need to be understood in the light of his other hymns. Second, as can be seen in most of the hymns quoted in this and the previous sub-sections, Nānak definitely holds the view that there is only One Reality, which

[74] *AG*, p. 843.
[75] *AG*, p. 943.
[76] *AG*, p. 1042.
[77] *AG*, pp. 25, 566, 661, 663, 876, 943, 1036, 1043, 1127, 1172, 1330, etc.

is absolute in nature, but which continues to pervade and live in the heart of every human being as well as in the rest of the universe. The relationship of Nānak's One Reality with this World will be examined in more detail in chapter four, but the next section will throw further light on this subject.

1.3.4. Nirālā

i. *Tu ekaṁkāru nirālamu rājā,*
Tü āpe savārihi jan ke kājā.
Amaru adolu apāru amolāku Hari
asathiru thāni suhāiai.
Dehī nagarī ūtamu thanā.
Panca lok vashi paradhānna.
Uppari ekaṁākāru niralamu sunn samādhi legāiā.
Dehī nagarī naū daravāje.
Siri siri Karaṇai sāje.
Desavai purakhu atītu nirālā āpe alakhu lakhāiā.[78]

You are the only One and also the unique King.
You take care of the affairs of people.
You are immortal, unshakeable, limitless, invaluable, and You Lord (Hari) are seated beautifully in your immovable place.
The best place is the town of the body,
where the five supreme virtues[79] live.
They are absorbed in the One, who is unique, through an absolute state of meditation.
The town of the body has nine doors,
The Creator has made these and fixed them. At the tenth door lives the (Supreme) Being (purakhu),
Who is wholly different as well as unique.
But the unseen Being makes Himself seen.

ii. *Āpe āpu upai nirālā saca thānu kio daiālā.*
pauṇ pāṇi aganī kā bandhanu Kotu rajāidā.
Naū ghar thāpe thāpnhāre dasavaiṁ vāsū alakkh apārai.[80]

[78] *AG*, p. 1039.
[79] The five virtues are Satu (Truth), Saṁtokh (patience), daū (mercy), dharmau (righteousness), dhiraju (steadfastness). Cf., Shackle, p. 178.
[80] *AG*, p. 1036.

He made (creation) alone, but kept Himself separate (from the world)
The Merciful One has established His true abode.
Bringing together air, water and fire,
He made the solid body of (human being).
The Creator also fixed the nine doors[81] to that.
At the tenth (door) unseen and infinite He Himself lives.

iii. *Ekama ekaṁkāru Nirālā*
Amaru ajonī jāti na jālā.
Agam agecaru rūpu na rekha
Khojta khojta ghatti ghatti dekhiā,
Jo dekhi dekhi dekhvai dekhavai tis kau bali jāī
Gura parasādi parama padu pāī.[82]

On the first day,
One, Absolute Being—unique, eternal, unincarnated, without identity,
Without impurity, inaccessible, imperceptible, without form or outline;
but through an ongoing search,
(I have) seen (Him) in each and every heart.
(I will) sacrifice for him, who will see (himself) and also make others to see.
By the favour of the Gurū, I obtained the highest status.

iv. *Joti joti samāṇī bhītari tā chode māiā ke lāhe.*
Saraba joti rūpu terā dekhiā sagala bhavana terī māiā.
Rarai rūpi nirālamu baithā nadari kare vicci chāiā.[83]

When light (of a human being) is absorbed in the Light, then attraction (of worldly wealth) is ended.
Among all lights is seen Your form,
The whole is Your wealth.
Among various worldly disputes and forms,
You are sitting separate, seeing mercifully the shadowy world.

[81] 'Ghar' can be translated as door or house.
[82] *AG*, pp. 838-9.
[83] *AG*, p. 351.

v. *Āpīnai āpu sājio āpīnai racio nāuṁ*
Duyī kudarati sājīai kari āsaṇu diṭṭho cāu.[84]

He fashioned himself gave Himself the Name.
Second, He made the creation, then seated himself and looks at it with delight.

The content of all these five hymns of Nānak is clear and does not need much explanation. These describe the relationship between 'the Absolute One' and 'the world'. In the first hymn Nānak affirms some of the important attributes of the 'One'. He addresses Him as 'You' (Tü), which states a very personal relationship. He says Tü 'ekaṁkāru nirālamu rājā', 'You are the only One and the unique King'. Here Nānak makes it clear that his 'One absolute Reality' is not just an abstract concept, it has a personal aspect toc. The use of the title 'rājā' (King) is an indicator of this fact, and also what he further says; 'You take care of the affairs of pcople'. In the same hymn Nānak lays further emphasis on the unique aspect of his 'One' by using still stronger expressions, 'ekaṁkāru nirālamu sunn samādhi lāgāi' (One who is unique through an absolute state of meditation), and atītu nirālā, i.e. literally 'wholly different and unique'. In the second expression, 'atītu nirālā', two strong phrases are used with the same meaning, which shows how much Nānak wanted to stress the point that his 'One' is certainly not identical with the world. The other notable points in this hymn are that Nānak addresses his 'One' with the title 'Hari' and locates His dwelling place in the human body at the tenth door (dasavai) which brings Him nearer to human beings. The use of the title 'purakhu' (Being) further stresses the same point. At the same time attributes related to his absolute or transcendental nature are also listed: immortal, unchangeable, limitless, etc.

The second hymn quoted above stresses the same point as the first hymn, but adds a further aspect of the relationship of the 'One' with the world: 'Āpe Āpu Upai', i.e. he alone made creation but still kept Himself separate (nirālā) from it. In this hymn it is recognized that the human body is formed out of air, water and fire, and yet this body enjoys the living presence of the unseen Lord and

[84] *AG*, p. 463.

Creator. Thus although the 'One'. who is Creator has a separate identity from the human being, even so there is a real possibility of relationship. It also states the fact that the Creator and humans are distinct, but there is a very close communion between the two.

The third hymn quoted above also affirms the same aspect of the 'One', his 'separateness' (nirālā), but makes it even clearer that Nānak's 'One' lives in every human heart (ghatti ghatti). The same point is stressed in the fourth hymn, but here Nānak sees the light (joti) of his 'One' pervading the entire universe. The phrases khojta, dekhiā, etc. (searching, saw, etc.) make it clear that all that Nānak says is based upon his personal experience.

The fifth hymn asserts still more forcefully the concept of Creator and creation. The Creator first made His own self with His identity (nāü), then very clearly Nānak says Duyī (second), different from Himself, He made creation (kudrati). Nānak also adds that the Creator looks upon his creation with delight.

It is clear that Nānak's 'One' is not the same as or identical with this world, but at the same time his 'One' also pervades, lives in and maintains His presence in the human being (dasavaiṁ, ghatti, saraba joti, etc.). In all the above five hymns Nānak has laid stress on the two aspects of his 'One', i.e. 'absolute-transcendent' and 'personal-immanent'.

1.4. OṀKĀR

Oṁkāri Bhahamā utapati,
Oṁkāru[85] *kīā jini citti.*
Oṁkāri saila juga bhāe,
Oṁkāri beda niramae,
Oṁkāri sabade udhare,
Oṁkāri guramukhi tāre,
Onama akkharu suṇhu bicaru.
Onama makharu tribhavaṇa sāru.[86]

Oṁkāri begot Brahamā.

[85] In the original text Nānak has used two spellings, Oṁkāri and Oṁkāru, with the same meaning.

This kind of variation is common in the *Ādi Granth.*

[86] *AG,* pp. 929-30.

Oṁkāru (is the One) who made the (human) mind.
Oṁkāri gave existence to mountains and ages.
Oṁkāri created Vedas.
Oṁkāri, that is, the Word, saved (living beings).
Oṁkāri saved the followers of Gurū.
Listen and meditate on Onama.
The eternal Onama is the essence of the three worlds.

Interestingly, this is the only hymn, in which Nānak has used Oṁkāru. But this hymn comes at the beginning of one of Nānak's very important works known as Dakhaṇī Oṁkāru. The hymn is written in the form of an acrostic, which was the usual form of poetry used in Nānak's time to express matters of serious importance.[87]

Here in this brief hymn Nānak has stated a number of important points about Oṁkār. First, Oṁkār is the Creator of Brahmā, who is considered to be the god of creation in Indian religious tradition. Oṁkāru is also the Creator of all the things that are seen in this world (e.g. mountains), including ages (jug). It is Oṁkāru who made the ancient religious books, e.g. Vedas. Oṁkār is also the saviour of living beings, and is worthy of worship.

In the last two lines of the above hymn Nānak has used Onama instead of Oṁkār. After describing all the functions of Oṁkār, Nānak addresses his readers or listeners: "Listen and meditate on (the syllable) Onama" and then he adds: "The eternal Onama is the essence of the three worlds."

But the question here to be raised is: Who is this Oṁkāru of Nānak? Nānak has to some extent hinted at the answer to this question, first, in his use of sabada with Oṁkār, and second, in the use of Onama in place of Oṁkār.

The meaning of sabada is sound or word.[88] The implied meaning of sabada is found in Nānak's Japu, where he says:

Kītā pasāu eko kavāu.[89]

(He) made the world's expanse with a, single saying.

[87] Talib: vol. III, p. 1903 (fn).
[88] S.V., 'Sabad' in Kahan Singh, p. 156. Apte, p. 907.
[89] *AG*, p. 3.

Here the phrase Kavāu means sound or word, which has been translated above as 'saying'.

Regarding 'Onama', there is no doubt that Nānak himself used it in place of Oṁkār and that, as Kahan Singh says, the relationship of Onama to Oṁkār is one of identity. Kahan Singh also gives Onama's other form, Oṁnamh or Oṁnam, i.e. salute to the Creator-protector. He concludes that Oṁkār is another form of 'OM' or Oṁ.[90] In fact, the fifth Gurū Arjan used Oṁ with exactly the same meaning as Nānak gave to Oṁkār in the above hymn. Gurū Arjan says:

> *Oṁ Guramukha kio akāra.*[91]
>
> Oṁ made all the forms, O Gurmukh.

From the above discussion it is clear that Nānak's Oṁkār in real fact is Oṁ or Om, which is regarded in the Indian religious tradition as the most sacred syllable. Om is an indeclinable "phonetic symbol, rather than a word".[92] But the point which should be noted here is that Nānak used Oṁkār in the above hymn instead of Om or Oṁ, and this is equally true of his use of Oṁkār in the Mūl Mantr. But does it make any difference? The answer is 'yes', because 'Om' is not a word or a verb or a noun, but is in fact a 'phonetic symbol' as Gispert-Sauch has put it. However when Kāra or Kāru is added to Om, it then becomes a masculine noun,[93] which implies that it refers to a personality or being. So here the meaning of 'kāra' is simply 'only', but this suffix changes the meaning and use of 'Om' both in grammar as well as in the hymns of Nānak.

1.4.1. Ik Oṁkār

The brief survey of translations and commentaries in Sections 1.2.1 and 1.2.2 of this chapter showed very clearly how the various translators and interpreters of the expression Ika Oṁkāru differ in their renderings and interpretations. One of the problems with the

[90] Kahan Singh, pp. 21-2.
[91] *AG*, p. 250.
[92] G. Gispert-Sauch: 'A Controversial Syllable', *Vidyajyoti* (May 1981), p. 233.
[93] S.V., 'OM', Monier-Williams, pp. 235-6.

works mentioned in these two sections (1.2.1 and 1.2.2) seems to be with the methodologies used in these works. Reference was made to Gopal Singh's conclusion and how he reached it.[94] In a similar way the earliest renderings included in our survey were those of Trumpps ('Om') and Macauliffe ("One God"). Both these scholars seem to have been influenced by the particular views which they held about Nānak. Trumpp was sure that Nānak "followed in all essential points the common Hindu philosophy"[95] of his day. Therefore it seems that he took it for granted that Ik Oṁkār is similar to the sacred syllable "Om" which is placed at the beginning of most Hindu scriptures.[96] Macauliffe held that the germ of the concept of the 'One' was obscured by the husk in the already existing religious traditions and that "Gurū Nānak, . . . gave expansion to this conception of the One God."[97] Those who have rendered Ik Oṁkāru as 'One God' (Macauliffe, Man Mohan Singh, Dewan Singh and Thiel-Horstmann) seem to have been influenced by the modern use of the term 'God', based on Semitic[98] and Christian concepts.[99] Other writers who used different phrases, but more or less with the same meaning, are Gopal Singh ("One Supreme Being"), Talib ("The Sole Supreme Being") Teja Singh (The One Supreme Being) Sohan Singh ("The One Universal Being"), Mcleod ("One Supreme Being") and these renderings are possibly closer to Nānak's thought. Among these translations, the oldest one is Teja Singh's (AD 1919), but how he arrived at his rendering, he has not explained. Of the others only Gopal Singh and Talib have given an explanation. References have been made to Gopal Singh already,[100] and according to the comments of Talib on Ik Oṁkār it seems he reached his conclusion by following the interpretations of Sant Mangal Singh (a Nirmala Sadhu) and Bhāī Gurdās. According to Sant Mangal

[94] Cf. p. 28. and Cf. p. 29.

[95] Trumpp, pp. XCVII, XCVIII, C.

[96] S.V., 'OM', Apte, p. 319 and Monier-Williams, p. 235.

[97] Macauliffe, vol. 1, p. LX (Introd.)

[98] Mohammed Marmaduke Pickthall (Trans.): *The Meaning of the Glorious Koran*, Delhi, 1986, p. 362.

[99] Cf. Dewan Singh, op. cit., p. 19.

[100] Vide, Sec. 1.2.1, p. 25.

Singh, Ik is "the manifestation of the Divine Essence" and "This (1) figure it is stated, is manifest in the form of Oṁkār, the Creator or attributed Brahm. Bhāī Gurdās in Vār 3.15 has given a central significance to Eka (One)".[101]

Among those who have made an attempt to interpret Ik Oṁkāru, Gurdās' view, which was given in Section 1.2.2.1, is the most important and original. He is the only one who has seen how Nānak's thoughts on Ik Oṁkāru developed. He saw that Nānak's Niraṁkāru, 'Formless', became ekaṁkāru, 'One', and then ekaṁkāru became Oṁkāru, 'the Word Sound', and then Oṁkāru became the agent of creation or Karatāru, Creator, as well as paravadagāru, the provider. Here a real attempt is being made to present Nānak's basic doctrine. This was discussed in Section 1.3.2., while stating Nānak's own view on Oṁkāru, in the well-known hymn at the beginning of Dhakaṇī Oṁkāru. In this Oṁkāru is the Creator, is worthy of worship, and is also the Saviour of all living beings.

Among the Panjābī language commentators, Gyānī Badan Singh, like Trumpp, almost ignored the figure "1" and equated Oṁkāru with the sacred syllable 'Om'. Even before his examination of Ik Oṁkāru he declared his theological position and affirmed that Nānak was an advaitin, one who upholds the doctrine of non-dualism. It is clear that Gyānī Badan Singh tried to interpret Nānak in the light of the existing philosophical traditions of his time (see Section 1.2.2.2).

Sāhib Singh and Bhāī Vīr Singh on the other hand tried to interpret Ik Oṁkāru by taking into account the literal meaning of the two words of this phrase. Sāhib Singh's stress is more on the aspect of the all-pervading presence of the Ultimate Reality (see Section 1.2.2.3). Bhāī Vīr Singh in his interpretation stressed the 'Oneness' (see Section 1.2.2.4), the meaning which he drew from "Ik" and "Oṁkār". He calls this Reality Mūl Hasti (Principal Being). Vinoba Bhave in his remarks about the figure "1" takes note of it and concludes that it refers to the Unity of God. For Vinoba Oṁkār is an important help in meditation. Here he has also accepted the traditional use of Oṁkār as a sound symbol as well as a syllable.

101 Talib: pp. XLVI-XLVII (Introd.).

But he accepts that Nānak has added a new flavour by using the expression Oṁkāru in his own way. Bhāī Jodh Singh more or less agrees with Bhāī Gurdās, because he says that Ik Oṁkāru represents the indescribable state of the "Formless" (Niraṁkāru) which was his before he became Creator (Sec. 1.2.2.5). In a way the methods and conclusions of the interpreters (tīkākāra) in Panjābī make a good beginning towards the understanding of Nānak's basic doctrine of the Ultimate Reality. But their attempts are mostly limited to the study of phraseology and are not based on the content of the hymns. For this reason the present work has made an attempt to study not only the phraseology, but also the content of the hymns. In fact, preference here has been given to the content of the hymns rather than to the literal meanings of various phrases used by Nānak.

The examination of the various hymns in Sections 1.3.1, 1.3.2, 1.3.3. and 1.3.4, under the heads (1) Ik Ekaṁkāru, etc., (2) Avaru Nā Dūjā, (3) Eka Mahi Saraba Saraba Mahi Eka, and (4) Nirālā throw sufficient light on what Nānak possibly meant by Ik or the figure '1'. It needs to be remembered here that Mūl Mantr is the essence of Nānak's teaching on the doctrine of the Ultimate Reality. That is why in the Mūl Mantr he used the figure "1" instead of the word 'one' which he used in his hymns written at different times and addressed to different audiences in different contexts. Nānak means the same thing by the repeated use of "eko" in his hymns[102] and by using the conceptual expression ekaṁkāru.[103] The repeated use indicates the stress which Nānak wanted to lay on the 'One' or 'Oneness'. The use of a title like Sāhibu (Lord) indicates that Nānak is not talking about some abstract concept, but instead means that his 'One' has personality or is a "Being".[104] The conceptual expression 'ekaṁkāru ' brings out the same idea, but still more forcefully. Here it should be noted that the expression 'ekaṁkāru' is certainly the handiwork of Nānak, and was coined possibly in order to stress the uniqueness and 'Oneness' of the Ultimate Reality. Ekaṁkāru is a masculine noun, which again refers to a personality or a male personality. The concept of "Being" is again stressed by its use. By dividing this phrase one gets two terms,

[102] Cf., p. 25.
[103] Cf., p. 26.
[104] Cf., p. 26.

ekaṁ and kāru. Ekaṁ means 'One' and 'kāru' means 'only'. So the simple meaning of this phrase is 'Only One', but because Nānak has used this phrase as a noun, it actually means "Only One Being". Then Nānak does not merely introduce this new title; he goes on to explain the nature of this 'Only One Being'. He says that this 'Being' is unique, eternal, unincarnated, without identity, without impurity, inaccessible, imperceptible and without form or outline. These qualities (guṇa) bring out another aspect of the nature of the 'Only One Being', i.e. that He is transcendent or absolute in nature. Of course the suffix kāru (only) also refers to the same truth. So the possible full meaning of ekaṁkāru is "One Absolute Being". Nānak also adds that he has found or has seen this Being's presence in every human being (ghati ghati). Moreover at the personal level he found himself in intimate and unbroken communion with this Being (eku samāī). This "One Absolute Being" he calls "parama tanta" (the Supreme Reality) and uses a number of other titles to stress both the "Absoluteness" as well as the "Oneness" of this 'One Absolute Being'. But at the same time Nānak laid stress on the all-pervading aspect (immanence) of this Being. The various titles applied to him like dātā (Giver), prabhū (Lord), karatā (Creator), pātisāhu (King), all emphasize his personal aspect and imply that there is a possibility of having a personal relationship with Him (see Sec. 1.3.1).

The expressions "avaru nā dūjā" (literally, "there is no second") and "eka tuī eka tuī" and "tisah sarīku na koi" (no one else is there to equal Him), all assert the existence of "One Absolute Reality". Here the point to be noted is that Nānak does not talk about 'unity'. The concept of unity only comes into the picture if there are more than one; but for Nānak there is only "One" and therefore the question of unity does not arise.[105] The expression "Avaru nā dūjā" and the other expressions all imply this. Again he addresses this "One" or "One Absolute Being", as "Paramesari" (i.e. the Supreme Lord; see 1.3.2).

The expressions "eka mahi saraba saraba mahi eka (All in One, One in all) and sohaṁ hamsā (He is I and I am He) as examined earlier in the light of Nānak's other hymns) emphasize the deep

[105] Cf., pp. 27-9.

communion that human beings can have with the "One Absolute Being". The basis of this deep communion is the all-pervading presence of the 'One' (see 1.3.3). The discussion of the expression nirālā (unique) in Section 1.3.4 further stressed the point that He is unique. All the hymns, which have been examined in this section bring out the fact that the unique Lord of Nānak is different from the things of this world. An expression like "purakhu atītu nirālā" (literally: "being wholly different, unique") makes it very clear that Nānak's "Supreme Being" is not identical with or similar to anything else. But at the same time the phrase dasavai (at the tenth door lives), refers to the other truth that "the unique being" of Nānak is present in the body of every human being. The expression "saraba joti" also makes the same point. But Nānak is definitely sure that there are two realities, Karatā and Kudarati.[106]

The well-known hymn examined in Section 1.3.2 under the head "Oṁkari" adds a further dimension to the "One Absolute Being". By using the expression Oṁkari Nānak has placed himself within the sphere of Indian religious traditions, in which this expression was already in use.[107] But Nānak's use of Oṁkāru differs from the existing religious uses of his time, because his Oṁkāru is the Creator of Brahamā, Veda, etc. Again the fact that Nānak's Oṁkāru is the Creator not only of this whole universe, but also of the gods, makes his Oṁkāru the Absolute, i.e. above everything. But Nānak's Oṁkāru is not only the Absolute or the Supreme in nature, he is also the Creator, the Protector, the Saviour and the One who can be worshipped. These facts make Nānak's Oṁkāru a personal (Being) also (see 1.3.2).

1.5. CONCLUDING REMARKS

Finally, what did Nānak mean by "1 (fig.) Oṁkāru"?[108] It is clear from the discussion in this chapter that this expression cannot be translated or rendered literally, but can be explained. The figure "1" preceding Oṁkāru cannot possibly be replaced with the word "one",

[106] Cf., p. 34.

[107] Colonel G.A. Jacob has listed in his Concordance more than 45 references from the Principal Upanishads and *Bhagavad Gita* (First Printed 1891, Delhi Edition, 1981, pp. 272-3).

[108] Cf. p. 15.

because it includes all the shades of the meanings contained in various expressions used by Nānak, like eko (repeated) ("only one"), ekaṁkāru ("One Absolute Being"), avaru nā dūjā ("no one else at all", or literally, "no one else second"), eka mahi saraba ("One in all") and nirālā ("unique"). The position of the figure "1" should be considered as emphatic, communicating the idea of "Absolute" or "Ultimate". So the possible rendering of figure "1" or "Ik" here can be "One Absolute . . .".

Again with regard to the term Oṁkāru which follows figure "1" — following the discussion in Section 1.3.2 and brief comments given at the end of the previous Section 1.4—it is clear that it cannot be replaced by the syllable "Om", nor can its meaning be taken as that which is found in the already existing religious tradition of Nānak's time. Nānak has, here, used it in the sense of a masculine noun, which confirms that he is referring here to a Reality which is 'personality' or even more correctly, a 'Being' which exists. Therefore the possible rendering of Oṁkāru here can be ". . . Reality" or ". . . Being".

So 1/Ik Oṁkār possibly means 'One Ultimate Reality' or 'One Absolute Being'.

CHAPTER TWO

Nāmu

2.1. INTRODUCTION

Besides the different names used by Nānak in his hymns for the Ultimate Reality, he used a special expression in the Mūl Mantr, satināmu, which needs special treatment in order to understand Nānak's concept of Name. The expression is a combination of two terms, sati and nāmu. The commentators on satināmu differ in their views about the relationship of sati and nāmu.[1] It is, therefore, important to examine the relationship of sati and nāmu at the beginning of this chapter.

Nāmu is also discussed in this chapter in the light of the phrases and terms used by Nānak and other Gurūs to express the concept of nāmu. Reference has already been made to satināmu (true name), which he used in the Mūl Mantr.[2] The other terms Nānak used are: asaṅkha nāva, innumerable names,[3] and akhari nāmu, name written in letters.[4] The fifth Gurū Arjan also used a similar term, which

[1] Pritam Singh (ed.): *Sikh Concept of the Divine,* Amritsar, 1985, pp. 9-13, 56-9.

Note: Dr. Ram Singh divided all the scholars who tried to deal with Satināmu into three classes.

1. Those who consider sat(i) as an attribute of nām(u) and render sat(i) nām(u) into English in a phrase like: "of the true name". They lay emphasis on nām(u).

2. Those who give more prominence to sat(i) than to nām(u) and translate sat(i) as "His name is Truth".

3. Those who lay equal emphasis on sat(i) and nam(u) and keep them apart as two distinct terms, neither of them qualifying the other; they translate sat(i) nam(u) as "Truth and Name".

[2] *AG,* p. 1.

[3] *AG,* p. 4.

[4] *AG,* p. 4.

clarifies the possible meaning of Nānak's akhari nāmu or satināmu. He says:

Kirtama nāma kathe tere jihabā,
Satināmu terā purā pūrabalā.[5]

The tongue utters the names of your attributes,
The true name is your primal and ancient name.

(Here it may be mentioned that on pages 1082-3 of the *Ādi Granth* Gurū Arjan gave a list of about 100 names.)[6] The tenth Gurū Gobind Singh used the phrase Karama nāmu, functional name,[7] in the same sense as Nānak used akhari nāmu and Gurū Arjan Kirtan nāma.

So it is very important for us to examine in depth the 'names written in letters', i.e. the 'attributive names' or 'functional names', in relation to 'the primal and ancient name'. In fact, the overall purpose of this chapter is to present a brief survey of the names used by Nānak, including satināmu, in order that this exercise may lead to a deeper grasp of his doctrine of the Ultimate Reality.

On the basis of the above introductory discussion, the theme of nāmu is dealt with under the following headings:

i. Sati and Nāmu: their relationship
ii. The meaning of Satināmu
  a. Sati
  b. Nāmu
iii. Asaṅkha Nāva

2.2. SATI AND NĀMU: THEIR RELATIONSHIP

In the text of the *Ādi Granth* the terms sati and nāmu are used together as well as separately. But it is important to note that in the Mūl Mantr satināmu occurs 43 times in different versions, including

[5] *AG*, p. 1083,
[6] *AG*, 1082-3: Karatā Ṭhākuru Gusāi, Prabhu, Pārabrahmu, Antarajāmi, Parmesaru Madhusūdanu, Suāmī, Hari, Krisana, Murāri, Jagjīvana, Narain, Banvārī, Ikku, Dātā, Deva, Nirañjana, Narahara, Sārthi, Rāma, Gupāla, Nirṁkara, Bānā, Gobinda, Isa, Pita, Nāthe, Satināma, Allah, Khudāi, Sukhdātā, Siva, Joti, Damodar, Bithula, Srīrang, etc.
[7] "Japuji" in *Nit-Nem* (Text with English translation) by Harbans Singh Doabia, Amritsar 1985, p. 60.

33 times the complete text.[8] This point is important, because of the unique place which Mūl Mantr has in the writings of Nānak.[9]

In his most important writing Japu Nānak used another form of Satināmu (sacu nai) both as one unit and also as separate words, as we see in the following:

i. *Sācā Sāhibu sācu nāi bhākhia bhāu apāru.*[10]

True is the Lord, true is the name,
his infinite love should be taught.

ii. *Soī soī sadā saccu Sāhibu sācā sācī nāi.*[11]

He is always Truth, the Lord is true and true is his name.

In both hymns Nānak used sācu nāi and sācī nāi in a masculine sense and we have, therefore, translated it as 'true is his name'. At the same time Nānak used Sācā Sāhibu, 'true Lord'. In the last Chapter (1.3.1), we have also seen that Nānak used the title Sāhibu in order to stress his point of the 'Oneness', eko, when he said:

Sāhibu merā eko hai[12]

My Lord is One.

Now the point which needs to be noted is that Sāhibu and Sāhibu's name are identical.

Sācā Sāhibu	=	Sācu nāi
True Lord	=	True name

There are other references in Japu which stress the same point even when Nānak used saccu and nāmu separately. The examples are:

1. *Ādi saccu jugādi saccu.*
hai bhi saccu Nānak hosī bhī saccu.[13]

[8] Footnote no. 35, p. 13.
[9] Cf., Chapter One, Sec. 1.1.
[10] *AG*, p. 2.
[11] *AG*, p. 6.
[12] *AG*, p. 350.
[13] *AG*, p. 1.

In the beginning was Truth,
In the beginning of the time was also Truth.
Truth is now and will be also.

2. *Jinhiṁ nāmu dhiāiā gae masakhati ghāli.*
Nānak te mukh ujale keti chutī nāli.[14]

Those who have meditated on the name have departed after putting in much labour.
Nānak, their faces will shine and many others will be liberated with them.

The first quotation is the opening sloka of Japu. Here Nānak uses saccu as a masculine noun, translated as 'Truth'. It is clear from the two previous hymns quoted, in which he uses sācā with the personal title Sāhibu that the sācā here refers to Nānak's Sāhibu.

The second quotation is part of the closing sloka of Japu. Here Nānak uses nāmu independently, though again as a masculine noun, nāmu dhiāiā (meditated on the name) which refers to the same reality, the reality to which Nānak makes a very clear reference in the opening sloka of Japu, i.e. saccu, and to which he also refers in the very first paüṛī,[15] when he raised the basic question concerning human need: "How can one be true (sacāru), how can the veil of false illusion be torn?"[16] So again it becomes clear that sometimes Nānak uses nāmu apart from saccu, but this use still refers to the same sense which he introduced in the Mūl Mantr through his combined phrase, Satināmu.

Besides Nānak, the fourth Gurū Rām Dās and fifth Gurū Arjan also used sati and nāmu together. For example Gurū Rām Das says:

Japi man sati nāmu sada sati nāmu[17]

O soul meditate on the true name, always the true name.

And Gurū Arjan says:

Sati nāmu terā purā pūrabalā.[18]

[14] *AG*, p. 8.
[15] paüṛi means stanza. Its literal meaning is applied to the step of a hymn ascending to a climax of praise.
[16] *AG*, p. 1.
[17] *AG*, p. 670.
[18] *AG*, p. 1083.

The true name is your primal and ancient name.

In other places Gurū Arjan says:

Sati nāmu parabhạ ka sukhdāī.[19]

The true name of the Lord is giver of comfort.

Even Gurdās in his vāra 24 has used sati and nāmu together when he says:

Sati sarup satināmu kari
satigura Nānaka Deva japāiā.[20]

By giving the form of the 'true name' to the Truth, Satigura Nānak Dev asked (us) to meditate on (it).

The discussion so far makes one point clear that sati and nāmu are normally used as one unit. It is also true that today this use is very common among Sikhs. In any Gurdavārā[21] 'satinām(u)' can frequently be heard on the lips of Sikh devotees. The same form is often used in the *Ādi Granth* by Sikh Gurūs as well as by other bhakatas.[22] Some of the examples are quoted in the next section.

2.3. MEANING OF SATINĀMU

In Section 2.2 it was seen that sati and nāmu, though two separate terms, are closely related to each other. We shall, therefore, first examine the meaning of satināmu as one unit, and then consider separately the meanings of sati and nāmu, in order to have a fuller grasp of this important expression. This section mainly deals with the views of different translators and commentators, which will help us to understand the problems related to this expression.

Trumpp: The true name is the creator.[23]
Macauliffe: There is but one God whose name is true.[24]
Gopal Singh: The Eternal.[25]
Man Mohan Singh: True is His name.[26]
Talib: Of eternal manifestation.[27]

[19] *AG*, p. 284.
[20] Gurdās 24.1.
[21] Gurdavārā means Sikh temple.
[22] Bhakatās means saints or devotees.
[23] Trumpp, p. 1.
[24] Macauliffe, vol. I, p. 195.
[25] Gopal Singh, vol. 1, p. 1.
[26] Man Mohan Singh, vol. I, p. 1.
[27] Talib, p. 1.

Teja Singh: Of the true name.[28]
Jodh Singh: If you want to name Him, call Him Sati (Satya).[29]
S.S. Kohli: His Name is Truth.[30]
Khushwant Singh: He is the supreme truth.[31]
Taran Singh: Reality, Reality of the appearance, Truth manifest.[32]

Monika Thiel-Horstmann has rendered satināmu in German as:

Sein Name ist Wahrheit.[33]

His Name is Truth.

Leading Punjābī commentators rendered the Satināmu as follows:

Gyānī Badan Singh: Karatā Purakhu īhām satināmu.[34]

The Creator being is the true name.

Sāhib Singh: Uh ek Oṁkāra, jis da nāma hai hond vālā[35]

He is ek Oṁkāra, whose name is having existence.

The above translators and commentators can easily be classified into four groups: first: Trumpp and Gyānī Badan Singh, who associated the satināmu with Karatā, the Creator, but their reasons for doing this are different. For Trumpp the reason is very simple: he gives no importance to the first term of Mūl Mantr (Ik) and further he takes the second term, Oṁkār, as equivalent to the Sanskrit term Om, which he regards merely as a sacred symbol at the beginning of Japu[36] (see chap. One, Sec. 4.) For him the Mūl Mantr only starts with "satināmu", and he, therefore, associated it with the term Karatā, and translated it: "The true name is the Creator".

[28] Teja Singh (Trans.): *Japuji*, Amritsar, 7th edn. 1974, p. 19.
[29] Jodh Singh: "Theological Concepts in Sikhism", *Religion and Society*, vol. XI, no. 1, March 1964 (Bangalore, CISRS), p. 33.
[30] Surinder Singh Kohli: *Philosophy of Gurū Nānak*, Chandigarh, 1980, p. 27.
[31] Khuswant Singh: *A History of The Sikhs*, vol. I, *1469-1839*, Delhi, 1986, p. 324.
[32] Taran Singh: "The Influence of Mūla Mantra on Gurbani", *Sikh Concept of the Divine*, ed. Pritam Singh, Amritsar, 1985, p. 128.
[33] Monika Thiel-Horstmann, *Leben Aus Der Wahrheit* (German), Zurich, 1988, p. 35.
[34] Farīdakota, vol.1, p. 2.
[35] Sāhib Singh, vol. I, p. 46.
[36] Cf., pp. 21, 22, 37.

Gyānī Badan Singh took notice of Ik '1' at the beginning of the Mūl Mantr, but could only see it as a veil before the sacred syllable Om. Therefore for him also the Mūl Mantr begins with Oṁkāru and ends with guraprasādi. Also, while commenting on satināmu along with Karatā Purakhu, he says that of that Being (purakhu), whose indicators are sati and nāmu, the same parmesura is the creator of the universe, which is the basis of nāmu.[37] In other words, according to him there is no difference between the Creator and creation, and satināmu refers to the Creator as well as creation, therefore his conclusion is that "Karatā purakhu īhāṁ satināmu" means "The Creator Being is the true name".

The first Sikh theologian Gurdās is also very close to this first group of thinkers, because he also associates satināmu more with Karatāru than with Ik Oṁkāru. This is clearly indicated in his Vāra 19.1.16; 22.1 and 39.1, where he says:

i. *Saccu nāmu Karatāru saci samāiā*[38]

The true name of the Creator is absorbed in Truth.

ii. *Saccu nāmu Karatāru gurmukhi pāiai.*[39]

The true name of the Creator one has obtained through the teaching of the Gurū.

Similar uses of saccu nāmu with Karatāru are found in Vār 22.1, but in 39.1 the form of saccu nāmu is satināmu.

The second group includes Macauliffe, Jodh Singh, S.S. Kohli and Monika Thiel-Horstmann. Their position is very clear. For them the Mūl Mantr begins with Ik and ends with guruprasādi and they understand sati as a noun. They have, therefore, translated sati with a capital 'T' as 'Truth'. Here the stress is on sati rather than on nāmu.

The third group includes Man Mohan Singh and Teja Singh. Here we have to note that both these scholars take sati as an adjective and nāmu as a noun and translate satināmu as 'true name'. In this rendering the stress on sati has been lost.

The fourth group, consisting of Gopal Singh, Talib, Khushwant Singh, Taran Singh and Sāhib Singh, prefer to paraphrase satināmu rather than to translate it. In this we can see a certain link with other

[37] Farīdakota, vol. 1, p. 2.

[38] Gurdās 19: 1.

[39] Gurdās 19: 16.

groups also. For example Talib and Taran Singh translate nāmu as 'manifestation' or 'manifest'. This rendering in fact refers to the creation and in this way both these scholars come very close to the first group, particularly Gyānī Badan Singh. On the other hand, Gopal Singh and Khushwant Singh have gone further in using paraphrases, particularly in their rendering of nāmu. Sāhib Singh has done the same with sati and has rendered it as "whose name is having existence".

All the different renderings of these translators and commentators make one point clear, that there is a serious problem in connection with this expression, satināmu. If one is going to depend only on literal translations, then it is going to be difficult to reach a reasonable understanding of this important expression. Therefore in the following two sub-sections an attempt is made to examine and understand the content of some of Nānak's hymns so as to arrive at some reasonable understanding of this expression.

2.3.1. SATI

i. *Ādi saccu jugādi saccu,*
hai bhī saccu Nānak hosi bhī saccu.[40]

In the beginning was Truth.
In the beginning of the time was also Truth.
Truth is now and will be also.

ii. *Saca khandu vasai Nirakāru.*[41]

In the realm of Truth the Formless lives.

The latter sloka is the second part of paüṛi 38 of Japu, to which reference has already been made. Also in Section 1.2 the following parts of two paüṛis of Japu 4 and 27 were quoted:

iii. *Sācā Sāhibu sācu nāi. . .*[42]

True is the Lord, true is the name. . .

iv. *Soī soī sadā saccu Sāhibu sācā sācī nāi.*[43]

[40] *AG*, p. 1.
[41] *AG*, p. 8.
[42] *AG*, p. 2.
[43] *AG*, p. 6.

There is always Truth, the Lord is true, and true is his name.

The above four quotations from Japu clearly show Nānak's view about sati or saccu, which are common Panjābī forms of the Sanskrit word satya. In these hymns Nānak not only refers to what he means by the term sati (which he placed in the Mūl Mantr after Ik Oṁkāru), but he also explains its relationship with Niraṁkāru (the Formless), Sāhibu (Lord) and nāmu (name).

In the first quotation Nānak three times uses saccu, which in Panjābī is a masculine noun. This is the reason why we have translated it as 'Truth' with a capital 'T'. This very fact indicates that 'saccu' is masculine in nature and has a personality. The second fact which becomes clear is that Nānak used 'saccu' three times to show its relationship with the three 'times', past, present and future. Saccu is present not only in all times, but also even before the reality of 'time' came into being. This is what Ādi indicates. So 'Truth' or saccu is that Being or Reality which always exists. This fact Nānak makes even more clear when he says above in the fourth quotation, 'sadā saccu', i.e. 'always Truth'. Thus saccu is 'eternal'.

Reference has already been made in the last chapter (1.2.2.1) to Niraṁkāru, 'the Formless', and here in the second quotation Nānak establishes the relationship of his 'Formless' with saccu. The place where 'the Formless' lives is sācā khandu, the realm of Truth. The point which needs to be noted here is that sācā khandu is the final stage of the human experience of the search for 'Truth' or 'Reality'. In the very first paüṛi of Japu Nānak raised the basic question which according to him concerns every human being. He asks: "How can one be true, how can the veil of false illusion be torn?"[44] After this question in Japu Nānak advances step by step, paüṛi by paüṛi, till he reaches almost to the end of Japu, and then he refers to sācā khandu, to the abode of 'the Formless'. Before this he has also mentioned other four stages—dharma khandu (the realm of righteousness), gianu khandu (the realm of knowledge), sarama khandu (the realm of efforts) and karama khandu (the realm of grace).[45] Through these four stages the human being gains those life experiences, or what are truly spiritual, or more accurately still,

[44] *AG*, p. 1.
[45] *AG*, pp. 7, 8.

mystic experiences, which lead him or her to the realm of Truth, where 'the Formless' lives. Here another point which can be noted is that 'the Formless', because of its very nature, cannot be experienced or known, but the fact of its being saccu, i.e..real, makes possible the experience of 'the Formless'.

On the basis of the above experiences, Nānak could address his 'Formless' with such personal titles as 'sācā Sahibu' and 'sācu nāi', 'True Lord' and 'True name'. In fact, according to these quotations sācā Sāhibu and sācu nāi, are the same.

There are many references in the hymns of Nānak according to which sācā,[46] sacra,[47] sācu,[48] sati, etc., have been used in a sense which is more than the simple meaning of the English term 'truth'. For example:

i. *Bāni būjhai sācī samāvai*[49]

He who understands the scripture is absorbed in the True (One).

ii. *Sacrā dūri an bhālīai . . .*[50]

Seek not the True (One) far . . .

iii. *Sati sati vartai gahira gaṁbhīra.*[51]

In truth, the true (One) pervades (all) in a deep mysterious way.

2.3.2. NĀMU

i. *Jeta kītā tetā nāmu.*
Vinu nāṁ vai nāhi ko thāṁu.[52]

As great is your creation, so great your name.
Without your name, there is no place.

ii. *Vadā Sāhibu ūṁcā thāṁu.*
Uṁce upparī ūṁcā nāmu[53]

[46] *AG*, p. 560.
[47] *AG*, p. 581.
[48] *AG*, p. 938.
[49] *AG*, p. 412.
[50] *AG*, p. 581.
[51] *AG*, p. 1023.
[52] *AG*, p. 4.
[53] *AG*, p. 5.

Great is the Lord, high is his place.
His name is highest above the high.

iii. *Sācā Sāhibu sācai nāi.*[54]

True is the Lord, true is the name.

iv. *Adrisat agocaru nāmu apārā.*
Ati rasu mitha nāmu piārā.[55]

The infinite name is unseeable and unknowable,
but extremely sweet is the beloved name.

These four stanzas from different hymns of Nānak present the inner nature of nāmu, Name.

Nāmu is often understood as a simple name. but here nāmu is equated in the first hymn with creation; in the second hymn namu's greatness is equated with the greatness of the Lord; in the third hymn Nānak directly equates nāmu with the Lord, Sāhibu. In the last hymn nāmu is shown as infinite and its other attributes are unseeable and unknowable. All these quotations tell us that Nānak's nāmu is more than a simple name, through which we can identify a particular person or thing. Rather, when Nānak uses nāmu, he is pointing to the Reality which is even beyond human sense.

In other places in the *Ādi Granth* Nānak talks about the unity or oneness of Nāmu. For example:

Ekā nāmu Eku nārāiṇu tribhavaṇu
Ekā joti.[56]

The One name, the one pervading reality (nārāiṇu)
in the three worlds, that is, the One Light.

Here in this hymn Nānak once again lays stress on the One Reality, the One Light, which is all-pervasive and this he calls 'eka nāmu'. The same truth about namū is found in the hymn quoted above, in which Nānak said: Vinu nāmvai nāhi ko thām̐u, i.e. 'Without your name, there is no place'. And of course the aspect of 'Oneness' is implied here also.

Nānak also addresses paramesaru, the Supreme Lord, concerning His name:

[54] *AG*, p. 9.
[55] *AG*, p. 1042.
[56] *AG*, p. 992.

Terā sācu nāmu paramesara,
Teri gati avīgati nāhi jānai,
aṇjaṇt nāma vakhāṇiāī[57]

O Supreme Lord, true is your name,
Your state is statelessness, which cannot be known,
But even though you are unknowable, yet cne has to take your name.

So Nānak continually lays stress on the 'one name' and the 'true name'. As his listeners were Panjābī villagers involved in agricultural work, he therefore uses their occupational language also to express the reality of the 'one name' and the 'true name'. For example, he says in one of his hymns:

Phasali ahārhī eku nāmu sāvanī sācu nāmu[58]

Spring harvest is the one name,
autumn harvest is the true name.

Here in the use of eku nāmu and sācu nāmu, one again hears an echo of the Ik which Nānak placed before Oṁkār (see Chap. 1, Sec. 1.3.1).

To make clear his concept of nāmu and its deeper meaning, Nānak used nāmu with both historical and attributive names belonging to different religious and sectarian groups. Some of the examples are:

Rāma nāmu[59]
Hari nāmu[60]
Nāmu khudāi[61]
Nāmu Narahari[62]
Nāmu Niranjanu[63]
Nāmu Murāri[64]
Nāmu terā Niraṁkāru[65]
Nāmu Karatāru[66]

[57] *AG*, p. 1168.
[58] *AG*, p. 1285.
[59] *AG*, p. 22.
[60] *AG*, p. 22.
[61] *AG*, p. 144.
[62] *AG*, p. 152.
[63] *AG*, p. 229.
[64] *AG*, p. 414.
[65] *AG*, p. 465.
[66] *AG*, p. 358.

Reference has already been made to sācu nāmu, nāmu apārā, sācu nāmu, nāmu Paramesra, etc. A detailed examination of these historical and attributive names will be undertaken in the next section, but here the point to be noticed is that for Nānak, nāmu is all-important; but the name may be Vaishnavite (e.g. Rāma, Hari) or Islamic (e.g. Khudāi), or non-Vaishnavite (e.g. Niranjanu), or non-sectarian (e.g. paramesara or Karatāru)—for him all are the same. But it is certainly nāmu which adds uniqueness to his doctrine of the Ultimate Reality.

Nānak's manner of demythologizing can be seen in his use of nāmu. For example in one of his hymns he says:

Brahamā Bisanu Mehesu saresat nāmi rate vīcāri[67]

Brahamā, Vishnu and Shiva have been exalted through deep meditation and absorption in the name.

How can one receive nāmu? Nānak answered this question in the following hymn:

Nānak nāmu milai kirapā Parabha to hoi.[68]

O Nānak, when the Lord shows his favour, one receives the name.

In another hymn Nānak says it is the Gurū who is the giver of nāmu:

Ammrit nāmu Gurū Vaḍadāna . . .[69]

The Gurū is the giver of Name-Nectar . . .

Sidha Gosaṭi is another of Nānak's important and richest writings. In this work (paüṛi 32-4) Nānak tells what happens to a person who gets absorbed in nāmu, and also the relationship of nāmu with sach and the role of the Gurū in relation to nāmu. Some lines of these paüṛis are given here as examples:

Nāme rāte haümaiṁjai.
Nāmi rāte saci rahi samāi. . .

[67] *AG*, p. 1013.
[68] *AG*, p. 905.
[69] *AG*, p. 941.

Nāmi rāte pāvhi mokh duāru . . .
Pūre Gura te nāmu pāia jāi . . .
Gura kai sabadi jo mari jīvai,
So pāi mokh duāru . . .
Nānak vadi se vadbhāgi,
Jinhiṁ sacu rakhia uradhāri.[70]

Absorbed in name, self-centredness comes to an end.
Absorbed in name, continue to remain absorbed
in Truth . . .
Absorbed in name, one enters the door
of salvation . . .
From the perfect Gurū, one receives the name . . .
By Gurū's word, one who dies, enters the door
of salvation . . .
O Nānak, One who keeps Truth fixed in the heart, is the most fortunate person.

In this hymn one important point becomes clear, namely, that nāmu, sabada and sācu are synonymous. Also the Gurū is the channel through which one receives these saving realities, which lead one to the door of salvation.

Concerning the creation of nāmu Nānak says in Vārā Āsā:

Āpinhai ā pu sājio āpinhai racio nāū.[71]

He himself created, and gave himself the name.

Nāmu or nāuṁ is certainly much more than an ordinary sabad of a Gurū—though in fact in the above hymns Gurū, should not be taken as a human Gurū, but as Ik Oṁkāru (see Sec. 1.3.2), who is also called pūre gurū or Parabū in the above quoted hymns. Again sācu, as well as sabada, in the above paüṛi of Sidha Gosaṭi should be understood in the same sense.

Nāmu in a real sense represents the total nature of Reality (Truth) and when conjoined with sati in a single word, satināmu, it presents the conceptual aspect of Nānak's Ultimate Reality.

[70] *AG*, p. 463.
[71] *AG*, p. 463.

2.4. ASAKHA NĀVA

2.4.1. Classification

Reference has already been made to Nānak's concept of Asaṅkha nāva, the innumerable names, and also to akhari nāmu, the names written in letters, which Gurū Arjan also addressed as kirtam nāmu, functional or attributive names. But at the same time Gurū Arjan gave satināmu as the primal and ancient name of the Reality (sati), i.e. of the Nānak's Ik Oṁkāru which Nānak himself addressed as 'sati namu' (see Sec. 2.1).

The subject of this section is the asaṅkha nāva or kirtama nāma. As the study of the primal name satināmu has led to a deeper understanding of Nānak's doctrine of the 'Ultimate Reality', in the same way a brief survey of the asaṅkha nāva as used by Nānak is given in this section with a view to seeing if it could lead to a deeper understanding of this basic doctrine. These efforts may also throw some light on the influences which might have contributed to moulding Nānak's thoughts.

Below is given the classification of all the names used by Nānak under the following four tables:

TABLE 1

Names (Sectarian and Non-Sectarian)

A. Hindu
B. Muslim
C. Sant & others

D. General
E. New

TABLE 2

Hindu (Vaishnavite) Names

A. Vishnu
B. Krisana
C. Rāma

TABLE 3

Names according to Language

A. Indo-Aryan
B. Arabic and Persian

TABLE 4

Attributive Names

Oneness	Absolute	Personal	Historical

Before commenting on these tables and classifications, it may be pointed out that the names included in these tables do not include those names which are merely adjectival in nature. Also that although great care has been taken in counting the names, there is still a possibility that there may be minor inaccuracies in these lists; and also in some cases the choice of names may look somewhat arbitrary. But all this will not prevent us from drawing reasonable conclusions.

2.4.2. General Comments on the Tables and Classifications

Table 1

Includes all the names used by Nānak in his hymns. These have been sub-divided into sectarian and non-sectarian, because in Nānak's time some of these were only used by particular major religious sects, while others in the course of time had come to be used by everybody. There are also names which are used for the first time by Nānak.

Section A: This section contains the names which were generally in use among Hindus.

Section B: This lists the names from Islamic sources.

Section C: In this section those names have been listed, which were in use among different sects, particularly the names which were in use outside the circles of Islam and the main groups of Vaishnavites.

Section D: This section includes either those names which were originally used by particular sects or religious groups, but later on had a much wider use. Many of these names are attributive in nature and were not related to a particular religious sect. This section clearly is the largest in size.

Section E: This section includes some of the new names which Nānak used. These include mainly the contextual names like Dariāu (river) and Kirasānu (farmer, in a Panjābī context), and those expressing the friendliness of Ik Oṁkār: Pritam and Priya (lover), Pati and Piru (husband), Sajjan (friend) and also Ekaṁkāru and Pūri (Only One Absolute Being and perfect).

TABLE 1: NAMES

SECTARIAN						NON-SECTARIAN			
A. HINDU		B. MUSLIM		C. SANT & OTHERS		D. GENERAL		E. NEW	
Banavārī	2	Allahu	2	(Ādi) Purakhu	39	Antarajāmī	2	Dariāu	1
Brahamu	33	Karīmu	2	Alakku	35	Ātamarāmu	10	Ekāṁkāru	13
Gobindu	7	Khudāi	12	Anāthu	3	Ātamahari	1	Kirasānu	1
Gosāṁi	3	Mīru	1	Bairāgī	3	Ātamarāu	1	Pati	6
Gupālā	6	Rahimu	1	Bhugatā	1	Bakhasanhāru	9	Piru	1
Hari	463	Sāhib	111	Gorakhu	1	Bidhātā	4	Prītamu	11
Jagadīsu	13			Gurūdeva	2	Bisranhāru	1	Prīyā	1
Jagannathu	1			Gurū	7	Dinī	1	Pūri	1
Jagadīsaru	1			Kentu	3	Dātā	39	Sahu	7
Krisanu	1			Khasamu	50	Dātāru	5	Sajjaṇu	10
Mādhu	1			Nāhu	1	Deva	3		
Madhusūdanu	1			Nāthu	19	Dekhanhāru	1		
Murāri	20			Nathnhāru	1	Dhanii	1		
Narahari	4			Nirabhaü	18	Dhuri	3		
Nārāiṇu	7			Niraṁjanu	58	Ekā	76		
Rāmu	219			Niraṁkāru	24	Hakku	2		
Siva	1			(Parama) Tattu	17	Ikkatu	1		
Srīdharu	1			Paramānandu	1	Īsaru	1		
Ṭhākuru	29			Parama Samjogi	1	Jagjīvan	5		
Vāsudeu	2			Sunnu	17	Jajmānu	1		
				Satiguru	8	Joti	22		
						Karaṇhāru	8		
						Karatā	62		
						Karīmu	1		
						Karatāru	22		
						Kātnhārā	2		
						Mitṇhara	1		
						Mohanu	2		
						Mūlu	2		
						Oaṁkāru	6		
						Onamu	2		
						Pārabrahmu	4		

TABLE 1: NAMES (*Contd.*)

SECTARIAN			NON-SECTARIAN		
A. HINDU	B. MUSLIM	C. SANT & OTHERS	D. GENERAL		E. NEW
			Paradhānu	5	
			Paramārathu	1	
			Paramātau	3	
			Paramesaru	9	
			Paravadagāru	2	
			Parkhanhāru	4	
			Prabhū	149	
			Pratipāḷā	2	
			Pātisāhu	16	
			Rahīmu	1	
			Rāi	1	
			Rājā	2	
			Rājanu	3	
			Rakhnhāra	3	
			Sacu	61	
			Sahanahāra	1	
			Sāhu	1	
			Siradāru	2	
			Sirandā	3	
			Sirjanhāru	17	
			Suāmī	9	
			Sujjanu	4	
			Sukhdātā	5	
			Sulatānu	5	
			Suratā	1	
			Tāranhāru	6	
			Veknahāra	1	
Total no. of Names: 20	6	21	59		10
Frequency of Occurrence: 815	129	309	618		52

TABLE 2: HINDU: VAISHNAVITE

A. VISHNU		B. KRISNA		C. RĀM	
Gosāṁī	3	Banavārī	2	Rāmu	229
Hari	464	Gobindu	7		
Jagadīsaru	1	Gupālā	6		
Jagadisu	13	Krisanu	1		
Jagannathu	1				
Narahari	4	Mādhu	1		
Nārāiṇu	7	Madhūsūdanu	1		
Srīdharu	1	Murāri	20		
Ṭhākuru	29	Vāsudeu	2		
Total no. of Names : 9			8		1
Frequency of Occurrrence:	523		40		229

TABLE 3: LANGUAGES

A. INDO-ARYAN		B. ARABIC & PERSIAN	
(Ādi) Purakhu	39	Allahu	2
Alakkhu	35	Bakhasanhāru	9
Anāthu	3	Darīāu	1
Antarajāmī	2	Hakku	2
Ātamhari	1	Karīmu	2
Ātamrāmu	10	Khudāi	12
Ātamrāu	1	Mīru	1
Banavārī	2	Paravadagāru	2
Bidhatā	4	Pātisāhu	16
Bisamhāru	1	Rahīmu	1
Brahamu	33	Sāhibu	111
Dānī	1	Siradāru	1
Dātā	39	Sirandā	3
Dātāru	5	Sultānu	5
Deva	3		
Dekhnhāru	1		
Dhanī	1		
Dhūri	3		
Eka	76		

TABLE 3: LANGUAGES (*Contd.*)

A. INDO-ARYAN		B. ARABIC & PERSIAN
Ekaṁkāru	13	
Gobindu	7	
Gorakhu	1	
Gurūdeva	2	
Gurū	7	
Gosāṁī	3	
Gupālā	6	
Hari	463	
Ikkatu	1	
Īsaru	1	
Jagadīsaru	1	
Jagadīsu	13	
Jagannāthu	1	
Jagjīvana	5	
Jajmānu	1	
Joti	22	
Karaṇhāru	8	
Karatā	62	
Karatāru	22	
Kātanhārā	2	
Kentu	3	
Khasamu	50	
Kirasānu	1	
Krisanu	1	
Mādhu	1	
Madhusūdnau	1	
Mitṇhāra	1	
Mohanu	2	
Mūlu	2	
Nāhu	1	
Narahari	4	
Nārāiṇu	7	
Nāthu	19	
Nāthanhāra	1	
Nirabhaü	18	
Niraṁjanu	58	
Niraṁkāru	24	
Oaṁkāru	6	
Onamu	2	
Pārabrahamu	4	
Paradhānu	5	

TABLE 3: LANGUAGES (*Contd.*)

A. INDO-ARYAN		B. ARABIC & PERSIAN
Paramānandu	1	
Parama Saṁjogī	1	
Paramārathu	1	
Paramātau	3	
Parama Tattu	17	
Paramesaru	9	
Parkhnhāru	4	
Pati	6	
Piru	6	
Prabhū	149	
Pratipālā	2	
Prītamu	11	
Prīyā	1	
Pūri	1	
Rāi	1	
Rājā	2	
Rājanu	3	
Rakhnhāra	3	
Rāmu	219	
Sahu	1	
Sāhu	7	
Sācu	61	
Sadanhāra	1	
Sajjaṇu	10	
Satigurū	8	
Sirajanhāru	17	
Siva	1	
Srīdharu	1	
Suāmī	9	
Sujjanu	4	
Sukhdātā	5	
Suratā	1	
Tāranhāru	6	
Ṭhākuru	29	
Vāsudeu	2	
Vekhanhāra	1	
Total no. of Names:	96	14
Frequency of Occurrence:	1716	168

TABLE 4: ATTRIBUTIVE NAMES

A. ONENESS		B. ABSOLUTE		C. PERSONAL		D. HISTORICAL	
Ekaṁkāru	13	Alakku	35	(Ādi) Purakhu	39	Banvārī	2
Eka	76	Allahu	2	Ātamarāu	1	Gobindu	7
Ikkatu	1	Antarajāmī	2	Bairāgī	3	Gopālā	6
		Anāthu	1	Bakhasanhāru	9	Jagadīsu	13
		Apāru	11	Bhugatā	1	Krisanu	1
		Bīnā	5	Bidhātā	4	Madhu	1
		Brahamu	33	Bisarnhru	1	Madhusūdanu	1
		Dānā	6	Dānī	1	Murāri	20
		Dhūri	3	Darīāu	1	Nārāiṇu	7
		Guṇi Gahiru	2	Dātā	39	Narahari	4
		Guṇi Nidhānu	3	Dātāru	5	Rāmu	229
		Hakku	2	Dekhanhāru	1	Siva	1
		Joti	22	Deva	3	Srīdharu	1
		Kādaru	3	Dhanī	1	Ṭhākuru	29
		Khudai	12	Gorakhu	1	Vāsudeu	2
		Mūlu	2	Gosāṁī	3		
		Nāthanhāra	1	Gurūdeva	2		
		Nirabhaū	18	Gurū	7		
		Niraṁjanu	59	Hari	464		
		Niraṁkāru	24	Īsaru	1		
		Oaṁkāru	6	Jagadīsrā	2		
		Onamu	2	Jagannāthu	1		
		Pārabrahamu	4	Jagjīvana	5		
		Paramānandu	1	Jajmānu	1		
		Paramārathu	1	Kantu	3		
		Paramātau	3	Karatā	62		
		Parama		Karaṇhāru	8		
		Saṁjogī	1	Karīmu	2		
		Paramesaru	9	Kartāru	22		
		Paramatattu	17	Kataṇhāru	2		
		Pūri	1	Khasamu	50		
		Sacu	61	Kirasānu	1		
		Sakatā	1	Miharvānu	1		
		Satigurū	8	Mīru	1		
		Sujjanu	4	Mitṇhāra	1		
		Sunnu	17	Mohanu	2		
		Vadadānā	2	Nāhu	1		
				Nāthu	19		
				Niramalu	5		
				Niravairu	1		

TABLE 4: ATTRIBUTIVE NAMES (*Contd.*)

A. ONENESS	B. ABSOLUTE	C. PERSONAL		D. HISTORICAL
		Paradhānu	4	
		Parkhnhāru	4	
		Parvadagāru	2	
		Pati	6	
		Pātisāhu	16	
		Piru	1	
		Prabhū	149	
		Pratipālā	2	
		Prītamu	11	
		Prīyā	1	
		Rabu	2	
		Rahīmu	1	
		Rāi	1	
		Rājā	2	
		Rājanu	3	
		Ramaīā	2	
		Sadnhāra	1	
		Sāhibu	111	
		Sāhu	7	
		Sahu	1	
		Sajjaṇu	10	
		Sarajītu	1	
		Siradaru	1	
		Sirjanhāru	17	
		Sirandā	3	
		Suāmī	9	
		Sukhdātā	5	
		Sultānu	5	
		Suratā	1	
		Tāranhāru	6	
Total no. of Names 3	36	70		15
Frequency of Occurrence: 90	384	1162		324

Table 2

Gives a further classification of names from Hindu sources, which were used in Nānak's time by one of the major sects, the Vaishnavites.
Section A: is a list of names of Vishnu.
Section B: gives various names of Krishna.
Section C: has the one name of Rāma, which was used by Nānak 229 times.

Table 3

This table includes a classification based on linguistic background.
Section A: lists 96 names, derived from Indo-Aryan languages.
Section B: lists the names which came from the Arabic and Persian background.

Table 4

This table classifies the names used by Nānak to express various attributes of the Ultimate Reality. It is important because it helps us to understand his view of the nature of the Ultimate Reality.
Section A: Three names mentioned here stress the 'Oneness' of the Ultimate Reality.
Section B: The names listed here reveal the other aspect of the nature of the Ultimate Reality, its absoluteness.
Section C: is the longest list of names, all personal in nature.
Section D: lists the historical names which were in use at the time of Nānak among various religious sects.

2.4.3 Conclusion Based on the Tables and Classifications

(A) The first thing which becomes clear simply from looking at Table 1 is the amazing variety of names which Nānak used for the Ultimate Reality. These names indicate the rich variety not only of his religious sources, but also of his linguistic sources. The function of these names is explained by Nānak from the outset in Japu. He says:

> *Akhari nāmu akari sālāha.*[72]

[72] *AG,* p. 4.

Through words (your) name is uttered, through
words (you are) praised.

This stanza makes it very clear that one has to address the Ultimate Reality in some verbal form and therefore Nānak uses different names according to the need and context. The following three examples from Nānak's hymns illustrate this point.

i. *Hariama jasu jacau nāmu,*
Gura parasādi Barhami samāu.
Painde aisa Barhama bicāru,
Name suci nāmo paṛu nāme cajju acaru.[73]
In place of a holy bath, I beg for Hari's name and praise.
By the grace of the Guru, I will merge in Brahaman.
O Pandit, meditate on Brahaman in such a way, that His name may be your purification, learning, wisdom and way of life.

ii. *Ta tü mulla ta tu kājī jiānhi nāmu Khudāi.*[74]

Then only you are a Mullah or Qazi, if you know the name of Khudāi.

iii. *Jo janu nāma Niraṁjan rātā,*
Nānak soi Purakhu Bidhātā.[75]
The Person who is absorbed in the name of Niraṁjan, he himself is the Purakhu Bidhātā (Lord Creator).

These three hymns show how Nānak used different names to convey the same thought to different groups belonging to different religious sects. Thus the first hymn is addressed to a Hindu Pandit (priest), and employs the appropriate names and religious expressions which the Pandit will understand. The second is very clearly addressed to a Muslim Priest, and here Nānak uses both the name and the religious expressions, which a Muslim will understand. The third hymn similarly is addressed to a Nātha belonging to a Sant

73 *AĞ*, p. 354.
74 *AG*, p. 24.
75 *AG*, p. 943.

religious tradition. Here again Nānak has used both the name and the religious expressions known to the Nātha. But all three hymns have the same theme, that of the Nāma or Name.

There are a number of other hymns in which Nānak has used different names from different religious backgrounds and languages with the same meaning. For example:

> Rāma nāmu,[76] Hari nāmu,[77] Nāva Khudāi,[78] Narhari nāmu,[79] Nāmu Niramjana,[80] Sāhibu nāi,[81] Nāmu Murāri,[82] Nāmu Nārāiṇu,[83] Nāmu Paramesaru,[84] Nāmu kartar,[85] Nāu Allahu,[86] etc.

So for Nānak names were not a problem, because he used all these names to express the same Reality. Gurū Arjan, the fifth Gurū, makes this point even more clearly, when he says:

> *Eko Allahu Parabrahama*[87]
>
> The Allahu (God in Islam) and Parabrahama (Transcendent Lord for Hindus are one and the same.

(B) Tables 1 and 2 also indicate another fact, that Nānak was certainly influenced by the context of his time. This influence is multi-sided and comes from different sources. According to the best known 'Janam Sākhīs' he travelled not only in India, but also to other neighbouring countries. He visited a number of religious places sacred to Hindus, Muslims, Buddhists, Nātha and Sant fol-

[76] *AG*, p. 22.
[77] *AG*, p. 22.
[78] *AG*, p. 140.
[79] *AG*, p. 152.
[80] *AG*, p. 229.
[81] *AG*, p. 249.
[82] *AG*, p. 414.
[83] *AG*, p. 992.
[84] *AG*, p. 1168.
[85] *AG*, p. 358.
[86] *AG*, p. 470.
[87] *AG*, p. 897.

lowers.[88] It was on his travels that he came in contact with people of different faiths and from these contacts he gathered the terms and names, which he later used when sharing his experiences and his fundamental teaching. This does not mean he created a kind of syncretism or mixture of the various influences which he received. On the contrary, he certainly had his own experiences, which are mystical in nautre, and this fact is seen in those writings which were written or to which he gave a final form during the last years of his life (see Introd. Sec. 3), particularly the Japu. In Japu he not only makes a selective use of names, but also reveals his deeper thoughts about the Ultimate Reality. It is in Japu that he speaks of the experience of his Niraṁkāru, the Formless One, on one side,[89] and on the other side he records his vision of the personal aspect of the same in the form of his Sāhib, the Lord.[90] It is significant that the most common names in Japu are either Sahib or Niraṁkāru. A third name which is commonly used is Niraṁjanu, meaning, utterly 'Pure'.[91]

(C) Again Table 1 brings out another point—Nānak's use of sectarian and non-sectarian names. Of sectarian Hindu names, only 20 names are used, but they occur more frequently (815 times) than any others. On the other hand, the largest number of names (59 names, occurring 618 times) are those which were in general use; these are given in Section D under the heading "Non-sectarian—General". Table 3 further indicates that among these the great majority are derived from Indo-Aryan languages, as opposed to

[88] (i) Bhāī Sāhib Doctor Bhāī Vir Singh Jī (ed.): *Puratam Janam Sākhī*, Amritsar, 1971 (7th edn.), pp. 60, 63, 182, etc.

(ii) Piār Singh (ed.): *Ādi Janam Sākhīs*, Jullunder, 1969, pp. 42, 73, 84, etc.

(iii) Kirapāl Singh (ed.): *Janam Sākhī Gurū Nānak Deva Jī* by Shrī Meharban, vol. I, Amritsar, 1962, pp. 130-50, 416, 449, etc.

(iv) Surinder Singh Kohli (ed.): *Janam Sākhī Bala*, Chandigarh, 1975, pp. 184, 186, etc.

(v) Kirapāl Singh (ed.) : *Bhāī Manī Singh Vālī Janam Sākhī*, Janam Sākhī Parampara, Patiala, 1969, pp. 330-401 (vide 342, 346, 249, 372, etc.).

[89] *AG*, pp. 4, 8.

[90] *AG*, p. 5.

[91] *AG*, p. 3.

Arabic and Persian. From these facts two conclusions can be reached. First, most of his contacts, as later on most of his followers, had on Indian background, and therefore the names and terms that he used were also adapted to the need of these people. Secondly, in his basic doctrine Nānak remained within the Indian tradition. For example, there are two names which are common to the Muslim religious tradition, Allahu and Khudai. For the Muslim, in fact, it is really Allahu (which is part of the first article of their creed), which is the basis of the Muslim doctrine of God in which the greatest stress has always been laid on His complete Unity.[92] However Nānak uses this name only twice in the first place he said Allah became the name of Khudāi (God).[93] In the other hymn he says that the Primal lord is called Allahu.[94]

(D) Table 4 Attributive Names: This is an important table, because reflection on the classification in this table will lead to a further understanding of Nānak's doctrine of the Ultimate Reality. Section A: includes three names with the same meaning, 'One', but the expression ekaṁkāru (see Chap.1, Sec. 1.3.1) lays the strongest stress on the aspect of 'Oneness' (ekaṁ = One and kāru = Only). All these names are used in the masculine gender, and refer to a personality.[95]

Section B: Here 37 names are listed, which can be further classified under the following sub-headings:

(a) Transcendent: Anāthu (without Master), Brahamu (Transcendental Being), Onamu (the Sacred Sound), Pārabrahamu (Supreme Transcendental Being), Paramatau (Supreme Reality), and Niraṁkāru (formless One).

(b) Absolute : Allahu (only One God), Bīnā (Omniscient), Dānā (all Wise), Dhūri (Primal Being), Guṇi Garhiru (treasury of deep Mertis), Guṇi Nidhānu (treasury of Virtues), Hakku (true Lord), Joti (Light), Kādaru (Omnipotent), Khudāi (Self-Existent God), Mūlu (Primal Being), Nirabhaü (Fearless), Niraṁjanu (Pure One), Nāthanhāra (Master), Oaṁkāru (Absolute Being), Paraumesaru (Supreme Lord), Pūri (Perfect), Sacu (Truth), Satigurū (True Gurū), Sunnu (Absolute Void), Sajjanu (Omniscient), and Vadānā (all Wise).

92 L. Bevan Jones: *The People of the Mosque*, Delhi, 1980, p. 84.

93 *AG*, p. 470.

94 *AG*, p. 1191.

95 *AG*, pp. 838, 904, 1039.

Section C: In this section 70 personal names are listed, which can be further classified under the following sub-heading:

(a) Creation: Bidhātā (Creator), Gorakhu (Lord of the world), Gosāmi (Lord of the Universe), Jagadīsru (Lord of the world), Jagjivanā (the life of the world), Karaṇhāru (Creator), Kartāru (Creator), Karatā (Creator), Kirsānu (Cultivator), Sirjanhāru (Creator), Sirandā (Creator), Sarjītu (Creator).

(b) Lordship: Rāu (Lord), Deva (Divine), Dhanī (Lord), Hari (God), Īsaru (Lord), Gurū (Teacher), Jagannāthu (Lord of the Universe), Jajmānu (Patron), Mīru (Lord), Nāthu (Lord), Paradhānu (Chief), Pātisāhu (King), Prabhū (Lord), Rabu (Lord), Rājā (King), Rājanu (King), Sāhibu (Lord), Siradāru (Chief), Suāmī (Lord), Sultānu (Emperor), Sāhu (Banker).

(c) Graciousness: Bakhasanharu (One who Pardons), Bisarnharu (Destroyer), Dāni (Giver), Darīāu (River), Dātā (Bestower), Dātāru (Provider), Dekhanhāru (One who Sees), Karīmu (Merciful), Kātanhārā (Destoryer), Miharvānu (Merciful), Miṭnhāru (Destroyer), Parkhuhāru (One who Examines), Pratipala (Sustainer), Rahimu (Merciful), Sadhanahāra (One who Calls), Sukhdātā (Giver of Happiness), Suratā (Listener), Tāranhāru (Saviour), Parvadgru (Provider).

(d) Relational: Bhugatā (Enjoyer), Purakhu (Husband or Man or Being), Kantu (Husband), Khasamu (Husband), Mohanu (Fascinator), Nāhu (Spouse), Pati (Husband), Piru (Lover), Prīyā (Lover), Sahu (Husband), Sajjanu (Friend), Gurū (Teacher).

(e) Personal but spiritual: Ātam Rāma (Beautiful Spirit), Ātam Rāu (Spirit Lord), Bairāgī (One who is away from the world), Gurūdeva (Teacher God), Niramalu (Spotless), Niravairu (Free from hostility), Ramaīā (Pervader).

Section D: In this section 15 historical names are listed, which are used by Nānak in his various hymns. Among these names 8 names are historically the names of various incarnations of Vishnu, 8 names of Krisna and one of Rāma (see Table 2).

According to one Hindu doctrine, that of the Trimurti, there are three gods or three aspects of the same supreme Reality—Brahama (creator), Vishnu (preserver), Siva (destroyer).[96] However Nānak includes these as part of the rest of creation:

[96] S. Radhakrishnan: *Indian Philosophy*, London, vol. I, 1951 (rpt.), pp. 480, 485, 517, 562.

He has made air, water, fire,
Brahama, Bisanu (Vishnu), Mahesa (Siva) and the creation[97]

Also Nānak's Ik Oṁkār or the Ultimate Reality is a jonī, that is, not conditioned by human birth, as he has very clearly stated in Mūl Mantr[98] and the same stress is found when he uses other titles, such as Brahaman ajonī. In fact, in the following hymn he has used at the same time both Brahaman who is the transcendent Supreme God, and Murāri, who is supposed to be Krisana (an incarnation):

So Brahama a jonī hai bhi honī ghatt
bhītari dekhu Murāri jiu.[99]

He, the Lord, who is not conditioned by human birth, is and also shall be.
Look within your heart, you see the Murāri (Enemy of pride).

Nānak also refers to both Krisna and Rāma in the plural along with Gopīes and Sītās as ordinary human beings, when he speaks of them as historical persons.[100] He even refers to ten incarnations of Rāma, but as created ones.[101]

The above discussion shows clearly that though Nānak used historical names known in his time to various religious sects, yet in reality he did not use them in their original settings; instead he applied them all to one Supreme Being or Reality. In fact, all the names he used have an attributive meaning in addition to their use for the Supreme Reality. For Example:

Banvārī (Creator or Life Giver to the forest, Gobindu (Creator or One who can be found through Bāṇi or Scripture), Gopūlā (Provider of the World), Jagadīshu (Lord of the world), Krisnu (Lord), Mādhu (Destroyer), Madhusūdanu (Destroyer of evils), Murāri (Destroyer), Narhari (Creator), Rāmu (All Pervader), Siva (Deity), Srīdharu (Lord), Ṭhākuru (Lord or Master) and Vāsudeva (All-Pervading God). Most of the above names are applied in the same way as the personal names (see Sec. C).

[97] *AG*, 504 (also another hymn *AG* 1037 and 1276).
[98] *AG*, p. 1.
[99] *AG*, p. 458.
[100] *AG*, p. 465.
[101] *AG*, p. 1276.

2.5. CONCLUDING REMARKS

From the whole discussion in the present chapter, one key point becomes very clear that though Nānak has used a wide variety of names for the Supreme or Ultimate Reality (Param tattu or Niraṁkāru), yet he, nowhere; allowed them to obscure in any way the absolute idea of Oneness, which he introduced in the Mūl Mantr as Ik Oṁkāru (see Chap. 1, Sec. 1.4). On the other hand Nānak used the variety of names to highlight the endless qualities of the Supreme Being (Oṁkāru or Paramesaru).

Secondly, if one has to choose one expression or title to express the wholeness of Nānak's concept of Absolute Truth or Reality, or the thought behind Ik Oṁkāru, it must be the Satināmu, which the fifth Gurū Arjan called purā pūrabalā, that is, the primal and ancient name. But Satināmu should be taken as a concept which explains what Nānak meant by his Ik Oṁkār.

Lastly, mention should here be made of one other well-known expression or name, which is very popular among the Sikhs, Wahigurū, which literally means wonderful Lord or Teacher. But as this name was never used by Nānak himself, it has not been included in our discussion. In the *Ādi Granth* this expression was used only by bards.[102]

[102] *AG*, pp. 1402-3.

CHAPTER THREE

Guṇa

3.1. INTRODUCTION

Already in chapter two (Sec. 2.4.3) much was said about the various attributes of the Ultimate Reality. In this chapter the meaning of the Guṇa will be discussed along with the main attributes which Nānak has listed in the Mūl Mantr. Two important aspects of Guṇa which are dealt here are : nirguṇa, literally without attributes, and saguṇa literally with attributes.

3.2. NIRGUṆA AND SAGUṆA

Most Punjābī scholars and other religious thinkers have agreed to call Nānak's hymns the beginning of the Punjābī Nirguṇu Kavi Dhārā, the Punjābī Nirguṇa Poetry Tradition. In fact, some of them even held that Nānak and other authors of *Ādi Granth* were basically believers in Nirguṇavad, i.e. those who believe that the Ultimate Reality is 'attributeless'. Their reasons for this conclusion are that Nānak and other Gurūs often used the term nirguṇa, and also that according to them Gurūs often used nirguṇa as a title for Brahama. But interestingly the examples quoted to support these arguments include along with nirguṇa, the other term saguṇa also.[1] For example they quote the following from Nānak

Niraguṇu te saraguṇu thia.

From attributeless form He took attributive form.

But the full verse to which these words belong is as follows:

Avīgatu niramāilu upaj niraguṇute saraguṇu thia.[2]

[1] Prem Prakash Singh: *Gurū Nānak Ate Nirguṇa Dhārā*, Patiala, 1973, pp. 6, 7.
[2] *AG*, p. 940.

From the formless state He assumed holy form,
From attributeless form He took attributive form.

In this hymn Nānak recognizes two states, nirguṇa and saguṇa, of the Ultimate Reality.

Nānak in a number of his hymns lays stress upon the truth that the Ultimate Reality has Guṇa. Some stanzas are quoted below in support of this argument:

i. *Nānak gāvīai guṇi nidhānu*[3]

Nānak, sing to him who is the treasury of virtues.

ii. *Akhari giānu gita guṇa gāi.*[4]

Through the words of songs your knowledge and attributes are praised.

iii. *Vade mere Sāhiba gahīrā gambhirā guṇi gahīrā.*[5]

O my great Lord, you are deep and profound and your attributes are deep.

iv. *Tere Guṇa kate?*[6]

How many are your attributes?

v. *Taü guṇa nāhī antu Hare.*[7]

There is no limit to your merits, O Lord.

In these quotations the important point to be noted is that in all of them Nānak is stressing the attributes of the Ultimate Reality, whom he also addresses with personal names, Sāhiba (Lord) and Hare (Lord).

The other important point to be noted is that Nānak only once used the terms nirguṇa and saguṇa and did so in one of his most important writings Sidh Gosaṭī, paüṛi 24 which has just been quoted. In this paüṛi, he used two very important phrases—avīgatu niramāilu upaj (from the formless state he assumed a holy form); and nirguṇu

[3] *AG*, p. 2 (also see *AG*, 21).
[4] *AG*, p. 4.
[5] *AG*, p. 9 (also see *AG*, p. 349).
[6] *AG*, p. 358 (also see *AG*, p. 359).
[7] *AG*, p. 990.

te saguṇa (from attributeless form He took attributive form). Nirguṇa here refers to avīgatu (imperceptible) and saguṇa to the later stage in which the Ultimate Reality can be experienced by a human being. In fact, what Nānak has done in his hymns is that he has treated these two states as attributes of the Ultimate Reality. The following two hymns from rāga soraṭhi are notable in this regard:

i. *Puṛu dhartī puṭu pāṇī āsṇu cāri*
Kunt caubārā . . .
Mere Sāhiba tere coj Vidāṇā.
Jali thali mahīli bharipuri līṇa ape
saraba samāṇā
Jaha jaha dekha taha joti tumārī terā rūpi kinehā. . .
Ikktu rūpe phirhi parachanna koi na kishi jeha.
Eku purabu maiṁ terā dekhia tū sabanā mahi ravantā.
Tere guṇa bahute maiṁ mūrakh kichu dījai.[8]

Upon land, upon water, in all the four directions is your seat and living place . . .
O my Lord, wonderful is your play.
You are omnipresent in ocean, earth and the sky.
You are also contained in all.
Wherever I look, there I find your light, How do you look?
You have only one form.
No one looks like another . . .
I have seen one of your wonders.
You dwell in all.
You have many attributes,
but I have not known even one.
I am a fool, O Lord give me some understanding.

ii. *Allakka apār agamm agocar nā tisu kālu na karamū.*
Jāti ajāti ajonī sambhaü nā tisu bhāü na bharamā sāce saciār vithu kurbāṇu.
Na tisu rūpa varanu nahī rekhiā sācai sabadi nīsan.
Na tisu māta Pita suta bandhap nā tisu kamu na nārī
Akula niraṁjan apar paramparu saglī joti tumāri.
Ghata ghata antari Brahamu lukāiā ghati ghati joti sabaī.[9]

[8] *AG*, p. 596.
[9] *AG*, p. 597.

He is invisible, infinite, inaccessible and imperceptible.
He is not subject to death and fate.
He has no caste, no birth but self-existence,
Without desire and doubt.
I am sacrificed to the truest of the true.
He has no form, no colour and no features.
Through the true Word his signs are revealed.
He has no mother, no father, no lust and no wife.
You O Lord, are without genealogy, pure, limitless and infinite.
Everywhere your light pervades.
In every heart the transcendent Lord is hidden and in every heart is His light.

Here in the second hymn Nānak gives a long list of the attributes which belong to the nirguṇa nature of transcendental Lord (Brahama)—invisible, infinite, inaccessible, imperceptible, above death and fate, without caste, without birth, self-existent, desireless, without doubt formless, colourless, featureless, motherless, fatherless, lustless, without wife, without descent, pure, limitless, etc.

But in the last two lines of this hymn Nānak shows what he means by the saguṇa nature of the transcendent Lord (Brahama). For this he uses the symbol of joti (light) and the all-pervading presence of Brahama, which pervades every point in the universe as well as every human heart.

The other point which Nānak here makes clear is that his concept of saguṇa is not to be taken as anthropomorphic or as resembling the concept of an avatār, in which the transcendent Lord comes down upon the earth in the form of a human being. He makes this clear by saying that he has no birth, but rather that he is self-existent. Also he has no human mother or father.

Nānak also says that all the attributes which belong to the nirguṇa nature of Brahama can be known through the true Word (sabad).

In the first hymn Nānak again stressed the omnipresent or all-pervading immanent aspect of his wonderful Lord (Sāhiba). Nānak sees that everyone in the universe is different and represents different attributes of his Lord. But still he does not fully understand even one of these, and therefore he prays for the wisdom to understand these attributes.

The point which needs to be noted here is that Nānak sees everything in the universe as representing some attribute or the other, because through his indwelling presence, the Ultimate Reality or Brahama shares his nature with his created world. Expressions like 'koi na kishi jeha'[10] (no one looks like another), 'Nānak karate ke Kete ves'[11] (so many forms of the Creator, O Nānak) express this point.

As regards the attributes belonging to the saguṇa nature of Brahama, another point that becomes clear from Nānak's hymn is that these Guṇa (attributes) are based on the experience of created beings in relation to their Creator. On the other hand the attributes belonging to the nirguṇa nature of Brahama are those which belong only to Him. The nirguṇa attributes include: His being one, omnipresent, invisible, inaccessible, imperceptible, unborn, self-existent, etc. Nānak has listed most of the nirguṇa attributes in the above two hymns from the rāga Soraṭhi. The following are some examples from Nānak's hymns of the saguṇa attributes:

i. . . . *Iku data* . . .[12]

. . . One bestower . . .

ii. *Nānak nadri Karami dati.*[13]

O Nānak, the gracious Lord
because of His favour He bestows gifts.

iii. *Devanhare kai hati danu.*[14]

The gift is in the power of the giver.

iv. . . . *tüṁ āpe melaṇhāru.*[15]

You are the uniter of man with Yourself.

v. *Tribhavaṇa tārnhāru suāmī eku.*[16]

The One Lord is the saviour of the three worlds.

[10] *AG*, p. 596.
[11] *AG*, p. 12.
[12] *AG*, p. 2.
[13] *AG*, p. 5.
[14] *AG*, p. 25.
[15] *AG*, p. 55.
[16] *AG*, p. 156.

vi. . . . *daiāla tūṃ.*[17]

You are merciful.

The examples of saguṇa attributes, which include bestower, giver, uniter, saviour, gracious, merciful, etc., can be quoted many more times from the hymns of Nānak, but these examples are enough to prove the above point.

Finally, to conclude this section, it can be said that nirguṇa and saguṇa represent the two sides of the same coin. These two aspects of the Ultimate Reality are (a) those which a human being can only affirm, the nirguṇa and (b) those which a human being can know or experience, the saguṇa. Gurū Arjan makes this very clear in his following hymn:

Niraṁkara akār āpe niraguṇa saraguṇa eka.[18]

The One Lord is without form, yet has form,
He is without attributes, yet with attributes.

3.3. GUṆA

Many references have been made to various guṇa (attributes) of the Ultimate Reality in previous chapters of this work, particularly in chapter Two (Sec. 2.4.3D) and in the previous section of this chapter (3.2). Nānak also listed some of the main attributes in the Basic Credal Statement (Mūl Mantr) which need special consideration. Two units of Mūl Mantr have already been discussed and examined in Chapters One and Two—Ik Oṁkāru and Satināmu. In this section we will now examine the following units, which contain the main attributes of Ik Oṁkāru or the Ultimate Reality:

i. Karatā Purakhu

ii. Nirabhaü Niraviru

iii. Akāla Mūrati

iv. Ajūnī Saibhaṁ

[17] *AG*, p. 422.
[18] *AG*, p. 250.

3.3.1. Karatā Purakhu

Different translators and commentators have translated or commented on these words, either separately or together as a unit and their renderings differ widely. For example:

> Trumpp: The true name is the creator, the Spirit without fear . . .[19]
> Gopal Singh: . . . Purusha, the creator . . .[20]
> Talib: . . . Creator, Immanent Reality . . .[21]
> Man Mohan Singh: . . . Creative His personality . . .[22]
> Gurū Iqbal Singh: Creator (of existence) Lord[23]
> Surinder Singh Kohli: A Purusha who is the creator[24]

Many other examples could be quoted to prove this point, but these six examples are enough for our purpose. In this section we will not examine the term Karatā, because it is going to have a full and detailed treatment in Chapter Four. Here our discussion will be limited to Purakhu (except that reference will be made to Karatā, when necessary). It is also clear from the above six references that there is less problem with the meaning of Karatā than with Purakhu. All the six translators have translated Karatā as the Creator (with a variation in the emphasis given to it—either less, as Trumpp, Man Mohan and Kohli, or more or equal, as Gopal Singh, Talib and Gurū Iqbal Singh).

However, almost all these translators have disagreed on the meaning of Purakhu: the Spirit (Trumpp), Purusha (Gopal Singh), Immanent Reality (Talib), His personality (Man Mohan Singh), Lord (Gurū Iqbal Singh) and A Purusha (Kohli).

The problem with the above translators is that they have mostly adopted only literal meanings. The term Purakhu is the Punjābī form of the Sanskrit term Purusha.[25] Purusha in Sanskrit has many

[19] Trumpp, p. 1.
[20] Gopal Singh, vol. 1, p. 1.
[21] Talib, vol. 1, p. 1.
[22] Man Mohan Singh, vol. 1, p. 1.
[23] Gurū Iqbal Singh, *Philosophy of Gurū Nānak*, Jodhpur, 1981, p. 2.
[24] Surinder Singh Kohli, *Philosophy of Gurū Nānak*, Chandigarh, 1980, p. 27.
[25] S.V., Kahan Singh, 'Purukhu', p. 777.

meanings. Some of these are: Man, Husband, Ruler, Spirit, God, Lord, King, Supreme Man, etc.[26] All that the above translators did, was merely to take one of these meanings, whichever they thought the best. Two of them have just replaced the Punjābī Purakhu with its Sanskrit form Purusha. It is, therefore, important to see what Nānak meant by using the term Purakhu. For this some of his hymns, in which he uses this term, are examined here:

i. *Tüm Karatā Purukhu agammu hai āpe Sristi Upātī,*[27]

You O Creator Purukhu, who are inaccessible, you yourself have formed the creation.

ii. *Ādi Purukhu aparamparu piār satigure slakku lakhāiā.*[28]

The True Gurū has shown me the Primal Purukhu
Who is different (from the creation) and is invisible.

iii. *Āpe agocaru purukhu nirālā.*[29]

The Purukhu himself is imperceptible and unmixed.

iv. *Tu akāla purukhu nāhī siri Kālā.*
Tu purukhu alekh agamma nirālā.[30]

You are the eternal Purukhu and death is not over your head. You are the incalculable purukhu (Being) and are also inaccessible and unmixed.

The above four hymns make a few fundamental points clear regarding Purukhu. The first hymn makes clear the relationship of Karatā (Creator) with Purukhu. In this hymn Nānak addresses Karatā Purukhu (as the cause of creation), who is also agammu (inaccessible). Here Nānak has definitely taken Karatā Purukhu as one unit.

Again in the second hymn Nānak introduces Purukhu with the word Ādi (Primal) and states that Ādi Purukhu is both invisible and different from the creation.

In the third hymn Nānak again speaks of Purukhu, as imperceptible and unique. In the last hymn Nānak declares that

[26] S.V., Apte, 'Purusu', p. 626.
[27] *AG*, p. 132.
[28] *AG*, p. 476.
[29] *AG*, p. 839.
[30] *AG*, p. 599.

Purukhu is eternal, not under the power of death, incalculable and inaccessible.

So in these hymns we see that Nānak uses Purukhu in the same sense and with the same qualification with which he uses a name like Parabrahamu Paramesaru,[31] the Transcendent Supreme Lord, or Allahu,[32] the One God.

The other important point about Nānak's use of the term Purukhu is that he sometimes uses it in a few hymns also in an ordinary sense. For example:

i. *Jinā satgurū rsi milai se pūre purakha sujāṇa.*[33]

Whom the True Gurū happily meets, they are perfect and wise men.

ii. *Narī purukha piāru . . .* [34]

The wife (woman) loves her husband (man).

Now keeping the above two sets of examples of hymns before us, we can say that in the first set Nānak uses Purukhu for the Karatā, (creator of the creation) whom he addresses as Ika Oaṁkāru in the Mūl Mantr.

The second set of hymns helps us to understand one other implication of Purukhu, in that it is a masculine noun, which represents the male human being. So a common person hearing Nānak's words must always have understood purukhu in this sense. Further we have to conclude that it was through the use of Purukhu that Nānak's listeners felt the nearness of Ika Oaṁkāru or the Ultimate Reality. When Nānak describes It as Satināmu, It is still abstract, though real; but when through the creative activity of Purukhu It comes close to human being then It becomes real, perceptible, accessible, etc.

3.3.2. Nirabhaū Niraviru

In the Mūl Mantr after dealing with the metaphysical and the personal or relational attributes Nānak then adds two important

[31] *AG*, p. 599.
[32] *AG*, p. 1191.
[33] *AG*, p. 22.
[34] *AG*, p. 148 (also see *AG*, p. 350).

ethical attributes of his Ik Oṁkār, nirabhaü and niraviru. Both of these attributes are taken together in one section, because in nature they are alike, being negative terms, and as a rule they are used together by Nānak in his hymns.

Where the meaning of these terms is concerned, most of the translators agree that these mean: without fear and free from hostility, respectively. These include:

Trumpp: Without fear, without enmity [35]
Macauliffe: Devoid of fear and enmity[36]
Gopal Singh: Without fear, without hate[37]
Man Mohan Singh: Without fear and enmity.[38]
Talib: Without fear, without Rancour.[39]

Though most of the translators and commentators (as the above examples show), agree about the meaning of nirabhaü and niraviru, there are still a few who do not agree with the above rendering, particularly with that of nirabhaü. Here two of them are mentioned.

Perhaps the first person who introduced a differnt shade of the meaning of nirabhaü was Gyānī Badan Singh. According to him the term nirabhaü is made up of two terms, nirabhava and nirabhaya. He further adds that nir means 'away or far' and bhava means 'because of illusion (maya) the created form of universe (includes what is seen the biggest and smallest)'; and in nirabhaya, nir means 'away or far' and bhaya menas 'fear'. For Gyānī Badan Singh these renderings imply that Sri Paramesawara is away from the illusory created world (He is not part of it), and also because He alone is eternal therefore he is away from the fear of death and other fear.[40]

The second commentator, who belongs to more modern times, is Gurū Iqbal Singh, who has also taken a stand very close to that of Gyānī Badan Singh. But he rejected outright the common view of most translators or commentators that nirabhaü means 'without

[35] Trumpp, p. 1.
[36] Max A. Macauliffe: *The Life and Teachings of Gurū Nānak* (1st Limited edn. 1903), Chandigarh, rpt. 1980, p. 239.
[37] Gopal Singh, vol. 1, p. 1.
[38] Man Mohan Singh, vol. 1, p. 1.
[39] Talib, vol. 1, p. 1.
[40] Farīdkot, vol. 1, p. 3.

fear'. He says the classical Sanskrit word nirabhaü has been mistaken for the word nirabhaya which means 'without fear or fearless'. He derives nirabhaü from the root 'bhav' which means 'becoming'; therefore the meaning of nirabhaü according to him is 'becominglessness'. He himself summarizes his discussion as:

> In short, the essence of all existence, the Being is 'without becoming'. The term 'nirabhaü' thus implies to what may be called the doctrine of becomingless of the Being. God is birthless and deathless.[41]

Where the meaning of niraviru is concerned, even these two scholars Gyānī Badan Singh and Gurū Iqbal Singh agree with others. Therefore before coming to the examination of niraviru, we will examine some of the hymns of Nānak, in which he has used the term nirabhaü. It is interesting to note that Nānak uses niraviru in only a few hymns, but in a number of his hymns he uses the term nirabhaü. These can be divided into four different categories; first, those in which Nānak speaks of nirabhaü (an adjective, but used as a noun) as his Lord, or uses it as a personal title. For example:

i. *Tuṁa gavhu mere nirabhaü ka sohila.*[42]

   You should sing a hymn of joy to my nirabhaü (Lord).

ii. *Nirabhaü siu liv lai*[43]

   I fell in love with Nirabhaü (Lord)

Then secondly, we have hymns, in which Nānak affirms that the Formless One or Lord is fearless. For example:

i. *Nirabhaü ape nirantari joti.*[44]

   (The Lord) Himself is nirabhaü and His light pervades everywhere.

ii. *Nānak nirabhaü niraṁkarū hori kete Rāma raval.*[45]

   O Nānak, the Formless One is (alone) nirabhaü,
   how many Rāma (or like Rāma) are like dust
   (as compared to Him).

[41] Gurū Iqbal Singh, op. cit., p. 14.
[42] *AG*, p. 12 (also see *AG*, p. 157).
[43] *AG*, p. 504 (also see *AG*, p. 1041).
[44] *AG*, p. 413.
[45] *AG*, p. 464 (also see *AG*, p. 465).

The third category of hymns connects bhai fear of the lord with nirabhaü. Example:

Bhai mā nai nirabhaü meri mai.[46]

One who lives in the bhai (fear of the Lord),
O my mother, becomes nirabhaü.

In the fourth set of hymns Nānak tells how human beings can become nirabhaü (fearless). Examples are:

i. *Ihu manu nirabhaü Gurmukhi nāme.*[47]

By meditating on the Name through the Gurū this soul can become nirabhaü (fearless).

ii. *Nirabhaü Satigurū hai rakhavalā . . .*
Nirabhaü so siri nāhī lekhā . . .
So nirabhaü gurū Sabadi pachānai . . .
Nirabhaü so abh antaru vasiā.[48]

The Nirabhaü, the true Gurū, is the protector . . .
He only is nirabhaü on whose head fate is not recorded . . .
He only is nirabhaü, who accepts the Word of the Gurū . . .
He only is nirabhaü, in whom (Lord) abides.

These four sets of hymns tell us: first, what Nānak himself meant by the term nirabhaü, and second (as of course is very clear already from the first three sets of hymns) that nirabhaü is an important attribute of Nānak's 'Formless One' or niraṁkārū. This is the reason why Nānak even addressed Him as nirabhaü, used as an independent title. Of course the second set of hymns, particularly the one quoted in which Nānak used nirabhaü with niraṁkārū, makes it very clear that this attribute belongs only to the 'Formless One', and therefore can be His title also.

Now to decide the meaning of nirabhaü. It is true that in Sanskrit we find the two roots, bhava meaning 'becoming', and bhaya meaning 'fear'.[49] But it should be noted that in every case in the

[46] *AG*, p. 1172 (also see *AG*, p. 18).
[47] *AG*, p. 415.
[48] *AG*, p. 1042.
[49] S.V. Apte, 'Bhava', p. 713 and 'bhaya', p. 711.

four sets of hymns, Nānak uses only one spelling for nirabhaü. It can also be seen that Gyānī Badan Singh stressed his first option (according to which he derived the second part of nirabhaü from the root bhava (becoming), and applied it to the whole created world, which according to him is not real) because he believed that Nānak was a Vedānti, one who believes only in one Reality (see Sec. 1.2.2.2), as he asserts in the very beginning of his commentary.[50] Gyānī Badan Singh was misled by his personal belief about Nānak, but in fact for Nānak this created world is not unreal, and the influence on it of māyā also has no place in his doctrine (see the detailed discussion below in chapter four). Therefore the first part of Gyānī Badan Singh's discussion, in which he derived nirabhaü from nirabhava, is not correct.

A second argument against Gyānī Badan Singh is drawn from the way in which Nānak uses the term nirabhaü. In the last hymn quoted above, it is very clear that Nānak is not talking about human birth (as both Gyānī Badan Singh and Gurū Iqbal Singh assumed). Then in the third set, Nānak talks about living in the fear (bhai) of the Lord, through which human beings can become fearless (nirabhaü). Basically this attribute of nirabhaü (the fearless) belongs to the Formless One (the niraṁkāru), but human beings can share in it through the means described in the last hymn quoted above.

About the second attribute, niraviru, there is no disagreement, as far as the meaning is concerned. All agree on 'without enmity', and even Gyānī Badan Singh[51] and Gurū Iqbal Singh[52] accept the same meaning in their commentaries. The attribute niraviru seems to be very closely related to the first one, nirabhaü. Nānak has, therefore, placed it in the Mūl Mantr immediately after nirabhaü. Even two instances of its use in his hymns, support this argument:

i. *Nirabhaü niraṁkāru niraviru pūran joti samāī*[53]

I am absorbed in the perfect light of the Formless One, who is fearless and without any hostility.

[50] Farīdkot, vol. 1, p. 1.
[51] Ibid., p. 3.
[52] Gurū Iqbal Singh, op. cit., p. 15.
[53] *AG*, p. 576.

ii. *Jugi jugi thāpe sadā niraviru.*
Janami marane nāhī dhandhā dharu.
Jo disai so āpe āpi.
Āpe upāī āpe ghat thāpe.
Āpe agocaru dhandhai loi.[54]

The Lord Who is without enmity (niraviru) is always stable throughout the ages.
He is not involved in any kind of strife or in the cycle of birth and death.
He Himself creates and establishes the body.
He Himself is beyond reach,
but the whole universe is busy with different works.

The first hymn makes it clear that the Formless One is free from any kind of fear and is also without hostility. This is because according to the second hymn, He is always stable, that is, He is the same at all times. He is not threatened by time, and is also beyond the reach of transmigration (birth and death), so that he has no fear of death. In fact, all that we see belongs to Him, having been created by Him; thus there is no question of His being involved in any kind of strife. Nānak makes it very clear in view of the above. He Himself is separate or beyond reach, and only created beings are involved in worldly affairs.

This hymn thus accounts for Ik Oṁkār or the niraṁkāru being nirabhaü (without fear) and niraviru (without hostility).

3.3.3. Akāla Mūrati

Akāla Mūrati is one phrase made up of two terms, akāla and mūrati, by the use of which Nānak describes the relationship of his Ika Oṁkāru with 'time' and 'death'. The first term akāla is used as an adjective qualifying Mūrati, which is the only feminine noun used in the Mūl Mantr. Most translators and commentators agree on the meaning of these terms, but it seems they had a problem as to which term, akāla or mūrati they should give more importance. Those who laid more stress on akāla connected it with 'time' while those who laid stress on mūrati connected akāla with 'death'. Some examples of these two groups are given below:

[54] *AG*, p. 931.

Those who laid stress on mūrati:

> Macauliffe: Immortal[55]
> Man Mohan Singh: Immortal His form[56]
> S.S. Kohli: A Being whom Death cannot assail[57]
> Sahib Singh: Whose form is away from death.[58]

Those who laid stress on akāla:

> Trumpp: Having a timeless form.[59]
> Gopal Singh: The Being beyond time.[60]
> Talib: Timeless Form.[61]

The above two groups agreed on the meaning of mūrati as 'Being' or 'Form', which is also its meaning in Sanskrit.[62] As regards meaning of mūrati taken together with akāla, Nānak has not in fact used these terms together in any of his hymns, But in two hymns he has added further depth to the meaning of mūrati:

i. *Sūkham mūrati nāma niraṁjan Kaia Kāākār . . .*[63]

   To (Him) whose form is subtle and whose name is niraṁjan, but creation is his body . . .

ii. *Terī mūrati ekā bhutu rūpu.*[64]

   You have one Form, but many (manifestations).

The first reference is actually part of a sloka after the fifth paüṛi of Āsā Dī Vār of Nānak. In this sloka Nānak comments on various religious sects. The stanza above quoted is part of his comment on those of the yogī and Natha sects who in a deep meditation concentrate on the name of unseen Creator, whose form is very

[55] Macauliffe, op. cit., p. 239.
[56] Man Mohan Singh: vol. I, p. 1.
[57] Kohli, op. cit., p. 27.
[58] Sahib Singh, pp. 64, 47.
[59] Trumpp, p. 1.
[60] Gopal Singh, vol. 1, p. 1.
[61] Talib, vol. 1, p. 1.
[62] S.V., Apte, 'mūrati', p. 768.
[63] *AG*, p. 466.
[64] *AG*, p. 1153.

subtle, which is imperceptible to the senses, but at the same time this whole universe is His body or form.

In the second reference quoted above Nānak sees 'One Form', Mūrati ekā, but everywhere in the universe he sees his numerous forms or manifestations.

So in the Mūl Mantr what Nānak really means by the term mūrati is that Ik Oṁkār or Niraṁjan's real form is very sūkham (subtle, imperceptible to the senses), but this Form can still be experienced through the created world.

The adjective akāla which Nānak added before mūrati has a very special place in Sikh religious thought. It is a terms to which Sikh Gurūs have given their own meaning. In Sanskrit akāla means wrong time or bad time or bad omen,[65] but it is not used in this sense in the Sikh Scripture. Nānak used it in addressing his Ik Oṁkāru or the Ultimate Reality. He says:

Tu akāla purākhu nāhī siri kāla.[66]

You are akāla Lord. On your head there is no death.

The tenth Gurū Gobind Singh wrote a complete work under the title Akāla Purukha,[67] which he used for the Supreme Reality or Ik Oṁkāru.[68]

Regarding the the meaning of Akāla, the two groups mentioned above differ in their translations. In the first group two of the translators contrasted it with the life of a human being who lived on this earth, and have, therefore, rendered it as 'immortal' (Macauliffe and Man Mohan Singh, see above) and the other two translators connected it with 'death' (Kohli and Sāhib Singh).

But on the other hand the second group which includes Trumpp, Gopal Singh and Talib rendered akāla with 'timeless' or 'beyond time', and have of course used this expression as a qualifying term with the mūrati (form). Now the implication of this term 'timeless'

65 S.V., Apte: 'akāla', pp. 3, 4.

66 *AG*, p. 1038.

67 Akāla Ustata, Siromani Guraduvārā Parbandaka Kametī Aṁritsar, 1969, p. 1.

68 Cf. ante, W.H. Mcleod: "A Sikh Theology for Modern Times", *Sikh History and Religion in the Twentieth Century,* ed. T. O'Connell et al., Toronto, 1988, p. 36.

is 'outside of time' or as Gopal Singh expressed it, 'beyond time'. The problem with the first view is less, because human death takes place within time or one can say it is a temporal reality. Therefore Ik Oṁkāru is from the point of time eternal, i.e. the limitations of time do not apply to Him.

But if we use 'timeless' for Ik Oṁkāru, as the second group has done, we are saying that He is timelessly eternal. The real problem here is not the 'time', the real problem here is the creation, particularly of human beings. By using this expression, akāla mūrati, Nānak is trying to explain once again the nature of Ik Oṁkāru in relation to the nature of human beings which according to him is not permanent or stable, and the tool which he is using to explain is 'time'. To reach a final conclusion, some of the hymns of Nānak have now to be examined, which deal both with the concept of the impermanence of human beings and creation, and also with the concept of time.

First, a few examples of hymns, in which Nānak deals with the theme of permanence:

i. *Thāpeā na jāi kītā na hoi.*
Āpe api niraṁjan soi.[69]

The Holy One is all Himself,
He is neither established nor created by any one.

ii. *Ādi anīlu anādi anāhadi jūgū jūgū eko vesu.*[70]

He is pure, primal, indestructible and has One form throughout the ages.

iii. *Asathiru Karatā dekhīai hora ketī āvai jai.*[71]

Only the Creator is seen to be permanent,
all others continue coming and going.

iv. *Sabh duni avanu jāvani mukāmu eku rahimu.*
Mukāmu tīs no ākhiai jīsu sisi na hovi lekhu.
Asamanu dharati chalsi mukāmu ohi eku.
Dīn ravi chalsi nisi sasi chalai tārikā lakh paloi.

[69] *AG*, p. 3.
[70] *AG*, p. 6.
[71] *AG*, p. 56.

Mukāmu ohi eku hai Nānak saccu bagoi.[72]

The whole world is coming and going.
Call him permanent, whose head does not have destiny written on it.
The sky and earth shall pass away,
He alone is permanent.
The day and the sun shall go,
the night and the moon shall depart,
and the hundreds of thousands of stars shall vanish.
he alone is permanent, Nānak tells the truth.

v. *Nā dinu raini na candu na sūraju sunna samadhi lagāidā.*[73]

There was neither day, nor night, nor moon,
nor sun, He alone sat in deep trance.

vi. *Rāti dinnatu Kie . . .*
Jotī jatī ganat na āve.
Jini saji so kimati pavai.[74]

He has created the night, day . . .
The numbers of lights and the kinds
which cannot be counted.
But He who has created them knows their worth.

The above six references make a number of points clear. The first hymn says that niraṁjanu, the Holy One, is self-established and also self-created; and the second hymn further adds that He always has an unchangeable form. In the third hymn Nānak asserts clearly that the Creator Lord is the only permanent Reality and that everything else is subject to the cycle of coming and going, that is, to change. In the fourth hymn Nānak tells us what he means by permanent or eternal. He says, "Call him permanent, whose head does not have destiny written on it." Here the term 'destiny' in the text is lekh, which means 'fate' or 'destiny'. It refers to the different stages of human life, including all that happens at each stage, until it ends with death. The continued possibility of change is part of every human life, and then comes the end, Now this life of ceaseless

72 *AG*, p. 64.
73 *AG*, p. 1035.
74 *AG*, p. 939.

change does not apply to the Creator Lord, who Nānak says is alone permanent or eternal.

The second main point which is clearly stated in the above hymns, particularly the fifth and sixth is that the Creator Lord, together with the rest of creation, also created day and night, sun and moon, which are the instruments by which time is measured and divided. In fact, this is the 'time' which is knownable to human beings and the indicator of change in human life. Then in the fourth hymn Nānak says that even day and night, sun and moon can depart or vanish, which means that measurable time is not permanent or stable or eternal, but only the Creator Lord is permanent. Here the question can be asked if there is such a thing as 'non-measurable' time; but Nānak is not concerned with this kind of question. The subject of his hymns is either the Creator or creation. What he says about the ever-stable nature of the Creator Lord and the continuously changeable nature of His creation, is limited to measurable time, which can be called 'temporal', referring to the different temporal categories, such as past, present, before, after, day, night, hours, months, years, forever, always, etc. And in relation to this Nānak uses the term akāla meaning 'temporally eternal' or 'one who is not affected by the above-mentioned limitations of time, including death'.

The third point which is clear is that it is doubtful if the term 'timeless' can be applied to Nānak's concept of 'eternity' or 'permanence', because it refers to a state, which would place the Creator Lord completely 'outside time or beyond time'. This would be possible only if it were accepted that Nānak believed in the doctrine of Non-Dualism. However, this was not his position, as we saw when discussing the question in chapters One and Two, and which will be reinforced by the discussion in the next chapter. Further, as was mentioned earlier, Nānak does not deal with the issue of time before the creation, except to affirm the absence of day, night, moon, sun, etc. His summary description of the pre-creation state is:

Arabada narabada dhundhūkarā.[75]

Millions and trillions of years ago all was deep darkness.

75 *AG*, p. 1035.

Once again, supposing that Nānak is referring here also to some kind of time-reality before creation, the expression he used, Arabada narabada (millions and trillions of years), simply refers to what is called above 'non-measurable time'. Of course this form of time-reality was existing already and can be an aspect of the Creator Lord's nature itself. But again it is going too far with mere assumption and therefore, terms such as 'timeless' or 'beyond time' cannot possibly be applicable to explain Nānak's doctrine of the eternity of the Creator Lord, or Ik Oṁkāru.

This section on Akāla Mūrati can perhaps be concluded by saying that Nānak affirms 'the eternity of the Form', and says that Ik Oṁkāru or the Creator Lord is above the limitations of the temporal state, to which every part of the creation, including human beings, is subject.

3.3.4. Ajūnī Saibhaṁ

Though ajūnī and Saibhaṁ are two attributes of Ik Oṁkār, yet as they are closely related in meaning as well as clarifying one another's nature, they are dealt with here under one head. Ajūnī is taken first because its examination will help us to understand the meaning of Saibhaṁ. This is also the order in which, in the Mūl Mantr and in the text of Nānak's hymns, these words are found. The following five important references from Nānak's hymns, including Mūl Mantr, may be a good starting point:

i. . . . *ajūnī Saibhaṁ* . . .[76]

. . . free from the limitation of human birth, self born.

ii. *Jāti ajāti ajonī sambhaü na tisu bhau Bharamā.*[77]

He without caste, ajonī and sambhaü, without desire and doubt.

iii. *Āpe atītu ajonī sambhaü Nānak Guramati so pāiā.*[78]

He is detached, ajonī and sambhaü,
O Nānak, He is found through the teaching of Guru.

[76] *AG*, p. 1.
[77] *AG*, p. 597.
[78] *AG*, p. 1042.

iv. *So Brahama ajonī hai bhi honi ghata bhitari dekhu Murāri jīu.*[79]

Brahama is ajonī and shall be also.
You should see Him in your heart as the enemy of pride.

v. *Gaganū agammū anā thu ajonī. . .*
Hari nāmu ceti phiri pavahi na jūnī.[80]

He is at the tenth door, inaccessible, without master, and ajonī.
If one remembers the Name of the Lord,
One will not again and again come to birth (jūnī).

In the above references the first point to be noticed is that in the one from the Mūl Mantr, ajūnī is spelt with the middle letter 'U', whereas in the other four references from Nānak's hymns, it is spelt with an 'O'. Also in the last hymn Nānak has used another important term, jūnī, which is spelt with the letter 'U'. This variation in the spellings can have a bearing on the problem of fixing the meaning of ajūnī or ajonī, and must therefore be kept in mind. But before beginning the analysis, some selected translations and commentaries are listed here, in order to see how they render or interpret these important expressions. These can be divided into the following groups:

i. The greater number of translators have rendered both ajūnī and ajonī as 'unborn'.
These include; Max A. Macauliffe,[81] Man Mohan Singh,[82] Teja Singh,[83] Surinder Singh Kohli,[84] Vinoba Bhave.[85]

ii. The second group consists of those who have rendered it as akārana, meaning 'without reason or cause'. These include Gyānī Badan Singh,[86] Bhāī Vir Singh.[87]

[79] *AG*, p. 598.
[80] *AG*, p. 932.
[81] Macauliffe, op. cit., p. 239.
[82] Man Mohan Singh, vol. 1, p. 1, vol. 6, p. 3040.
[83] Teja Singh, *Japuji*, Amritsar, 1974 (rpt), p. 19.
[84] Kohli, op. cit., p. 27.
[85] Vinoba Bhave, *Japujee* (Hindi), Varanasi, 1965 (revd edn), p. 34.
[86] Farīdakot, vol. 1, p. 3.
[87] Vīr Singh, 1981, p. 29.

iii. The third group rendered it as 'not produced from the womb' or 'Un-Wombed'. This group includes Trumpp,[88] Gurū Iqbal Singh,[89] Wazir Singh.[90]

iv. The fourth group consists of those who have rendered both ajūnī and ajonī as 'Unincarnated' or 'Not-incarnated' and 'one who does not take birth' (not incarnated in human form). These include Talib,[91] Gopal Singh,[92] and Jodh Singh.[93]

v. There are some other interpreters who have not taken a very clear stand, but include almost all the above meanings in their explanations, e.g. Jagjit Singh Saluja,[94] and Sāhib Kaur.[95]

vi. There is also one commentator in Panjābī who has rendered the expression ajūnī as 'one who is free from transmigration' or without birth or death.[96]

So we see that there are a number of possible renderings and interpretations of ajūnī and ajonī. But what did Nānak actually or possibly mean when he said Ik Oṁkār is ajūnī or ajonī? It may be helpful to look into the meaning of this expression first in Sanskrit (from which this term is taken) and then also into its usage in Panjābī.

In its Sanskrit form, the term is ayonī, which is a combination of a + yonī. The perfix 'a' means 'not';[97] and 'yonī' means womb

[88] Trumpp, p. 1.
[89] Guru Iqbal Singh, op. cit., pp. 2, 17.
[90] Wazir Singh, "Sikh Concept of the Divine", in Pritam Singh, ed., *Philosophy of Mūla Mantra,* Amritsar, 1985, p. 143.
[91] Talib, vol. 1, p. 1, and vol. III, p. 1909.
[92] Gopal Singh, vol. IV (rev.), p. 945.
[93] Jodh Singh, *Ajūnī in Sikh Concept of the Divine,* ed. Pritam Singh, op. cit., pp. 99, 106.
[94] Jagjit Singh Saluja, *Mūl Mantr* (Punjābī), Ludhiana, 1982, pp. 164, 180.
[95] Sahib Kaur, *Sikh Thought,* New Delhi, 1986, pp. 6, 17, 18.
[96] Sahib Singh, p. 47.
[97] S.V., Apte, 'a', p. 1 and also S.V., Monier-Williams, 'a', p. 1.

or vagina, or any place of birth or origin, or a generating cause, or a family, stock, race, birth, or form of existence.[98] So the literal meaning in Sanskrit is 'not (from) womb' or 'not (from) vagina', or 'not (taking) the form of existence or race or family, etc.' [99] The point here to be noted is that 'yonī' in Sanskrit is used in two senses or meanings: (a) a generating cause (organ) and (b) a race or form of existence. But this is not the case in Panjābī. In Panjābī 'yonī' is a common word for 'womb' or vagina,[100] and 'jūnī' is the word used for form of existence, or birth, race, etc.[101] So in Panjābī, yoni or joni are commonly used for 'the cause of birth' or 'the birth'; an juni for race, family, etc. The perfix 'a' has the same meaning 'not', as in Sanskrit. So we must now see in which spelling and with what sense, Nānak has used the word in his hymns.

Here it will be good to go back to the beginning of this section, where five references from Nānak's hymns are quoted. There it was noted that in the Mūl Mantr, the term used is ajūnī, whereas in his hymns Nānak used ajonī. We also noted the interesting fact that the last hymn no.V) uses the term ajonī in the first line, and in the last line, jūnī. We may first ask why Nānak used different spellings, one in the Mūl Mantr and the other in the hymns. To this one answer may be that the final arrangement of the text of the *Ādi Granth* was completed by Gurū Arjan, for which he took the help of Bhāī Gurdās. The spelling which we find in the Mūl Mantr is the one which was regularly used in the writings of both Gurū Arjan[102] and Bhāī Gurdās.[103] Possibly therefore the spelling in the Mūl Mantr was simply the one which Gurū Arjan used in his own hymns. Otherwise in Nānak's hymns the spelling of ajonī is completely consistent.

[98] S.V., Apte: 'yon', p. 789.

[99] S.V., Apte: 'ayoni', p. 143.

[100] S.V., *Punjābī Kosha*, vol. V, 'yonī', p. 355 (Also Teja Singh, *Anglo-Punjābī Dictionary*, Ludhiana, 1964, 'vagina', p. 530 and 'womb', p. 559).

[101] S.V., *Punjābī Kosha*, vol. II, 'jūni', p. 552. (Also Vide *Punjābī Sabada —Rup Te Sabada—Joṛ Kosa*, vol. IV, Punjābī University, Patiala, 1983, p. 149 and Teja Singh: op. cit., p. 57.)

[102] *AG*, pp. 99, 916, 1082, etc.

[103] Gurdās, 3.15, 39.1.

The above variation in the spelling of ajonī may also have been responsible for the different translations and interpretations of ajonī. For example, Sāhib Singh (Group VI) took the common usage of Punjābī of ajūnī and interpreted it as 'jūnam tuṁ rahīt' or 'Jo janam vic nahīm auṁada' ('One who is free from transmigration' or 'one who does not come to birth'). This rendering is based on the meaning of Jūnī as birth in the cycle of 84,00,000 classes of animate beings in which human beings continue to come and go on the basis of their actions done during the lifetime.[104]

Now to consider the position of first group, which included Macauliffe, Man Mohan Singh, Teja Singh, Kohli and Vinoba Bhave, who rendered both ajūnī and ajonī as 'unborn'. If we keep in mind the above discussion, particularly of the meaning of ayoni as used in Sanskrit, we may understand how they arrived at this meaning. Their rendering will be one possible meaning based on its meaning in Sanskrit, particularly the second meaning mentioned above.

The second group of interpreters rendered ajūnī or ajonī as 'without reason or cause'. Here again the meaning of jonī or yonī in Sanskrit as seen above helps us to see how they arrived at the above meaning, according to which yonī (womb or vagina) is the cause or reason of human birth. Thus they are possibly following the first meaning which Sanskrit offered above.

The third group, which included Trumpp, Gurū Iqbal Singh and Wazir Singh, rendered ajūnī as 'not produced from the womb' or 'Un-Wombed'. Trumpp has explained in his footnote, how he arrived at his rendering. He took ajūnī as a + jūnī (free from the womb) and has given a meaning to a = not, jūnī = womb, and further understood sambhau as the Sanskrit word sambhava meaning birth or production. So he concluded that it means 'not produced from the womb'. But Trumpp is too literal, in his rendering and we have also to see if his understanding of sambhaü as sambhava is correct or not. This will be discussed later on. Wazir Singh in his explanation has added more confusion by using the expression 'not cast in the womb'.[105] In this he also comes close to the first group. Gurū Iqbal

[104] *Punjābī Kosha*, vol. 2, p. 552.
[105] Wazir Singh, op. cit., p. 148.

Singh took the literal meaning of jonī as 'womb', and translated ajūnī as 'Un-Wombed'. In this explanation he is close to the fourth group, because ajonī is the basis on which he proves that Nānak, through this argument, has "rejected the theory of re-incarnation".[106]

The fourth group translated both ajūnī and ajonī as 'unincarnated' or 'not incarnated'. It is true that one of the implied meanings of ajūnī or ajonī will be that Nānak's Ik Oṁkār does not take any form or incarnation, because He is above the process of birth and death,[107] and so there is no question of his coming as an incarnation in any form. Therefore, as far as this implied meaning is concerned, this group is right to fix the definite or essential meaning of ajūnī as 'unincarnated'. In this they also gain support from Punjābī usage.

Before taking up the examination of Saibhaṁ it will be good to conclude our discussion of ajūnī and ajonī. On the basis of what has been said above, the first point which becomes clear is that the right expression to consider here is ajonī (not ajūnī), which was consistently used throughout the hymns of Nānak.[108] Also we have seen that the meaning of ajonī is 'without generating cause'. Nānak himself refers to the fact that every being in this world (except the One True Lord) is born of 'woman', as he says in his famous Āsā Dī Vār:

Bhandhu hi bhandu ūpajai bhandai bājhu nakoi
Nānak bhande bāharā eko caccā soi.[109]

From a woman is born a Woman,
Without a woman none is born Nānak,
only the True (Lord) is not born of woman.

The above hymn makes it very clear what Nānak means by his concept of ajonī, in connection with the True Lord or Ik Oṁkār, that his existence does not depend on 'woman' or jonī or yonī. In another hymn Nānak stresses the same fact still more powerfully, where he says in Vār Malār Kī:

[106] Gurū Iqbal Singh, op. cit., p. 17.
[107] *AG*, p. 597.
[108] *AG*, p. 489, 597, 598, 838, 1042, 1255.
[109] *AG*, p. 473.

Nā tisu bāpu na māi Kini tū jaiū.[110]

He has no father or mother.
Who has given You birth.

In these hymns Nānak does not deny that Ik Oaṁkār has a form of existence of birth; all that he states is his wonder, how Ik Oṁkār came into being or existence. One thing is absolutely clear, namely, that it was not through the natural process of birth or through the womb or from a mother and father. The term which he used to refer to the form of Ik Oṁkār's existence is ajonī, which cannot be rendered or translated by a single English term. It only can be explained as has just been done. However, Nānak has clarified the meaning of ajonī by adding after this term another phrase, Saibhaṁ. The answer to Nānak's question is found in this second expression. But what does this mean?

In understanding the meaning of Saibhaṁ, there is less difference among the translators and interpreters. Most of those who have translated it into English, have rendered it as 'self-existent';[111] but strangely the Panjābī interpreters have rendered it as saiparakas[112] (self-illumined). On the other hand Trumpp renders it as 'produced' (produced from the womb).[113]

As Trumpp is the earliest translator, this discussion will therefore begin with him. Mention has already been made of his rendering of Saibhaṁ on which he has again taken his own line. He explains in his footnote how he arrived at his rendering. He takes Saibhaṁ

[110] *AG,* p. 1279.

[111] Some of those who rendered saibhaṁ as 'self-existent', are:
Macauliffe, op. cit., p. 239.
Teja Singh, cp. cit., p. 19.
Gopal Singh, vol. IV (rev.), p. 945.
Talib: vol. 1, p. 1.
Kohli, op. cit., p. 27.

[112] Some of those who rendered saibhaṁ as sai-parakas means self-illumined, are:
Farīdkot, vol. 1. p. 3.
Vīr Singh, 1981, p. 30.
Sahib Singh, p. 47.
Jodh Singh (ed.), *Gurū Nānak Bani* (Panjābī), New Delhi, n.d., p. 17.
Man Mohan Singh, vol. 1, p. 1.

[113] Trumpp, p. 1.

as the equivalent of another Sanskrit term, sambhaya, which means 'birth' or 'production'; and on the basis of the latter sense he translated Saibhaṁ as 'produced'.

Those who rendered Saibhaṁ as 'self-existent', adopted a different derivation of this term, understanding saim as svayaṁ meaning 'self' or 'his own',[114] and bhaṁ as bhü, that is, 'being' or 'existent'.[115] It is clear from this derivation and interpretation why Saibhaṁ has been translated as 'self-existent'.

As regards the third rendering, 'self-illumined', or in Panjābī, sai-parakas, both Bhāī Vīr Singh and Sāhib Singh have given a different derivation which explains how they arrived at this meaning. According to Bhāī Vīr Singh,[116] the first part saiṁ or sva in Panjābī is equivalent to sai or svayaṁ in Sanskrit, meaning 'his own', while bhu = bha in Sanskrit means 'to shine'.[117]

Now which of the renderings or derivations offered by different translators and interpreters is correct? Here again one can look at the text of some of Nānak's hymns (see hymns II and III) at the beginning of this section in which he has used sambhü; in other hymns he uses expressions which convey the meaning of this word. Of course, as this term has its root in Sanskrit, its meaning in that language can also help towards a decision, but at the same time the discussion, of ajonī in the earlier part of this section should also be remembered.

The spelling used in the Mūl Mantr is Saibhaṁ (Saibhaṁ),[118] while in the text of Nānak's hymns it is sambhaü.[119] Once again, as in the case of ajonī, the spelling in Mūl Mantr is close to or identical with that which the compiler of the *Ādi Granth Sāhib,* Gurū Arjan[120] and his assistant Gurdās[121] used in their writings. So to

[114] S.V., Apte: 'svayaṁ', p. 1018.
[115] Ibid., p. 721.
[116] Vir Singh, 1981, p. 30.
[117] Apte: S.V., 'bhü', p. 714.
[118] See Prologue, p. 15.
[119] In the discussion the spelling, which Nānak uses in the text of his hymns is mostly followed, sambhaü; the other spelling saibhaṁ is only used where needed either when referring to Mūl Mantr, or to any translator or commentator who has used this spelling.
[120] *AG,* p. 99.
[121] Gurdās, 39.1.

some extent this change in spelling has misled the translators and interpreters in their renderings or interpretations.

As was shown above the meaning of ajonī is without generating cause or without father and mother. Thus its use does affirm a birth, but not one like that of a human being. Then what does it actually refer to? The answer lies in the meaning of sambhaü, which is derived from two originally Sanskrit words Sam or svayaṁ ('self') and bhaü or bhu ('to be'), which when joined together mean self-existent[122] or 'self-born'. So Nānak's Ik Oṁkāru is ajonī, meaning that His birth is not like human birth in its cause or its process. In this case the cause and process of His birth is His own self. Therefore he is 'self-born' (not Un-born). He is 'self-caused' (not 'without cause', akārna). For this sense support can also be found in Nānak's hymns. The most well-known example is in Āsā Dī Vār, where he says:

Āpīnai āpu sajiō,
āpīnai rcio nau.[123]

The Lord Himself created His own self,
He also took His own Name.

3.4. CONCLUDING REMARKS

Ik Oṁkār, or Brahama, or the Ultimate Reality, is full of attributes; in the words of Nānak, He is Guṇi Nidhānu (treasury of virtues). These virtues or attributes are deep and profound, and therefore Nānak calls guṇī gahīrā (deep attributes). These attributes are divided into two groups: (a) those which reveal the absolute and also the transcendent nature of Ik Oaṁkāru. Such attributes human beings can only affirm, because they belong only to Ik Oṁkār himself. They include: being One, omnipresent, omnipotent, invisible, infinite, inaccessible, imperceptible, birthless, self-existent, etc. Because these cannot be perceived by human senses, they are called in human language nirguṇa, but in fact this term does not mean an absence of guṇa or attributes. (b) those which reveal the personal nature of Ik Oṁkāru. These attributes are the direct result of human experiences of the Creator, Ik Oṁkāru. These include: bestower,

122 S.V., Apte: 'svayaṁ-bhü', p. 1018.
123 *AG*, p. 463.

giver, saviour, merciful, gracious, etc. These are known as saguṇa.

The basic attributes of Ik Oṁkār are: Creator (Karatā), personal being (purakhu), without fear (nirabhaü), without hostility (niraviru), eternal (akāla) and selfborn (sambhaü). Two of the guṇa, mūrati and ajonī, can only be described, because of the difficulty in finding an equivalent in English. The nearest rendering of mūrati is 'being' or 'form'; and ajonī means 'one who is free from the limitation of human birth', because he is 'self-born', saibhaü.

The above basic guṇa exemplify the two aspects of the nature of Ik Oṁkār, (a) absolute: nirabhaü, niravira, akāla, ajonī, sambhaü, and (b) personal: Karatā, purakhu, and mūrati.

CHAPTER FOUR

Karatā

4.1. INTRODUCTION

In the last chapter, the basic guṇas of Ik Oṁkār, as listed in the Mūl Mantr, have been discussed; but one of the basic guṇas, Karatā, was left to be discussed in this chapter. Karatā is undoubtedly a basic guṇa, because this is the attribute, which establishes the primary relationship at the personal level between Ik Oṁkār and His created world. Nānak's concern in his hymns is not, in fact, to expound a systematic concept of the Creator and creation, because he is basically a religious mystic. All the discussions in his hymns arose out of various personal human needs, including his discussion of the concept of the Creator and creation. The basic concern or question with which Nānak was faced, is related to a universal human need as he has stated in Japu. He says:

Kiva saciārā hoiaia, Kiva Kuṛai tutai pāli.
Hukami rajāī calanā Nānak likhiā nāli.
Hukami horani ākāru hukamu na Kahiā jāi.[1]

How can one be true, how can the veil of false illusion be torn?
Nānak, it is by obeying His will according to His order (command), which is already written in our being.
By His order (command) the creation came into being,
But His order cannot be described.

This is part of the opening stanza of Japu, the first book of the Ādi Granth. It reveals the basic concern of Nānak, which he raised in the form of a question: How can a human being be true or how best in the words of Teja Singh, can he be 'justified'?[2] How can the veil

[1] *AG*, p. 1.
[2] Teja Singh, *Jap Ji*, Amritsar, 1974, p. 19.

of untruth or falsehood or false illusion be removed, which has come in between Ik Oṁkār and human beings? The answer, according to Nānak, is by keeping or obeying His Order or command, which is pre-ordained. Here one needs to take note of this word, His Order, Hukami, because it is repeated in the following stanza (quoted above) in which Hukami is the agent of creation. Hukami is a link between Ik Oṁkār (who is Karatā according to the Mūl Mantr) and ākāru (creation, which includes human beings). Reference will again be made to this hymn later on, but here the point which needs to be made clear is that Nānak's starting point is a personal concern or need, and that can be satisfied only by the same agent which was originally responsible for the human being's creation, that is, hukami.

The references to Creator and creation, which one finds either in the form of short verses or long hymns describing the process of creation, occur in the context of matters of even greater concern to him. But in these passages Nānak has given much material, which reveals the nature both of the Creator and of His creation, and also their relationship. In the next section we will analyse Nānak's creation hymns.

4.2. MAIN CREATION HYMNS AND THEIR ANALYSIS

4.2.1. Hymns

i. *Arabada narabada dhundhūkārā.*
Dharṇi na gaganā hukamu apārā.
Na dinu raini na candu na suraju suna samadi lagāida . . .
Brahamā Bisanu Mahesu na Koī.
Avaru na disai Iko soī . . .
Na Ko ākhi vakhānai dūjā.
Āpe āpi upai vigasai āpe Kīmati pāidā . . .
Na tadi Gorakhu na maccindo . . .
Beda Kateba na simmriti sāsāta . . .
Kahatā bakatā āpe agocaru āpe alakhu lakhāida . . .
Ja tisu bhāṇā ta jagatu upāiā.
Bājhu Kalā ādāṇu rahāiā.
Brahamā Bisanu Mahesa upae māiā mohu vadhāida.

Virale ku guri sabadu sunaia kari kari dekhai hukamu sabāiā.
Khand Brahamand pātāl aranabhe gupatahu paragatī āidā.[3]

Millions and trillions of years ago there was only deep darkness.
There was neither earth nor sky;
(Only) the infinite (Being's) will was there.
There was no day, no night, no moon, no sun;
(Only He) was there in an absolute state of meditation ...
There was no Brahma, Vishnu or Shiva.
Except the One, no one else was seen there . . .
There was no talk or mention of a second (duality).
He (the Lord) rejoiced in giving existence to Himself;
and He alone evaluated Himself . . .
There was no Gorakh nor Machinder . . .
There were neither Vedas, nor Semitic Books, nor Simirtis nor Shastras . . .
The (Lord) Himself was speaker and preacher,
He, the imperceptible and Unseen, Himself saw everything.
When he willed, He made the world;
and without any support stretched out the vast expanse.
He made Brahma, Vishnu and Shiva;
Also He aroused the attraction toward Maya.
A few He made to hear the Word.
He made the creation and sees it;
And His Order ran through the Universe.
He divided the Universe into continents and under-worlds.
Thus from the unmanifest, He became manifest.

ii. *Suna Kalā aparampari dhārī.*
Āpi nirlāmu apara apārī.
Ape Kudarati Kari Kari dekhe sunnhu sunnu upāidā.
Pauṇu pānī sunnai te sāje.
Sirasathi upāi Kāiā gara raje . . .
Sunnhu Brahama Bisanu Mahesu upāe.
Sunne varate juga sabāe . . .

[3] *AG*, pp. 1035-6.

Sunnhu candu suraju gainare.
Tis Kī joti tirabhavan sāre.
Sunne alakha apara niralamu
sunne tārī lāida.
Sunnhu dharati akasu apāe.
Binu thammā rākhe sacu Kalapāe.
Tirabhavan sāji mekhulī maiā api upāē Khapāida . . .
Sunnhu upajī sunni samāmī.
Utabhuju calatu Kīā siri Karatai
bisamadu sabadi dekhāidā . . .
Ape Kāranu Kia aparampari sabhu tero Kīā Kamāida.[4]

The Absolute (Lord) in His unattributed state was (there) with His might.
He Himself remained unique, separate and boundless;
He Himself with his might made the creation
and saw it, and from the void He made the void sate, from the unattributed void fashioned air and water.
And after making the world, and in the fortress of the body, He became the Ruler . . .
From the unattributed void were made Brahma, Vishnu and Shiva.
From the unattributed void all the ages came into existence . . .
From the unattributed void came into existence the moon, the sun and the firmament.
His light pervades all the three worlds.
The unseen, infinite and unique (Lord) in His unattributed state was there in His unbroken trance.
From the unattributed void were made earth and sky;
And with His true might He protected them without pillars.
He created the three worlds and also (to bind them together) fashioned the rope of Maya[5]. . .
From the unattributed void they came into existence and in the same they will merge.
The Creator made and displayed the creation (utabhuju),

[4] *AG*, pp. 1037-8.
[5] Māyā here means worldly delights, which appear as real, but are actually corrupting (Shackle, p. 237).

and through His Word He has shown the wondrous show . . .
The Absolute Lord Himself caused it all;
and all worked out perfectly according to His Will.

iii. *Āpe sacu Kia Kāra jori.*
Aṇḍaja phoṛi joṛi vichori.
Dharati akāsu Kīe baisaṇa Ku thāu.
Rati dinantu Kīe bhau bhau.
Jini Kīe Kari Vekhanhāre . . .
Avaru nā dūjā sirajaṇahārā.[6]

He Himself truly made (the creation) by joining (all),
By breaking the Egg He joined and unjoined them.
He made the earth and sky and places to live.
He made night and day and (along with these also) fear and love.
He who made the creation, also takes care of it.
(Of the creation), no other one (except Him) is the Creator.

4.2.2. ANALYSIS

The three hymns quoted above agree in most details except for the beginning of creation, which is a very important factor for understanding the nature both of the Creator and of creation. Therefore these hymns need systematic analysis, which will be carried out under the following three heads:

i. Dhundhūkārā (Deep Darkness)
ii. Sunnu (Void)
iii. Aṇḍaja (Born of Egg)

These three phrases also echo concepts of creation, belonging to the earlier religious traditions of India which will also be referred to in our discussion.

4.2.2.1. *Dhundhūkārā*

This Dhundhūkārā creation hymn is the most popular and most often quoted hymn of Nānak. Almost all the scholars who have in some way dealt with this concept of Nānak have referred to this

[6] *AG*, p. 839.

hymn.[7] A similar hymn is also found in the *Rigveda*[8] and scholars refer to that hymn as a source for the doctrine of creation 'out of nothing'.[9] According to the Purāntan Janama Sākhī[10] Nānak composed this hymn during his third journey (AD 1515-17), in which he visited Kashmir. Before this journey Nānak had already travelled in the North as far as Assam (AD 1497-1509), and also to the South as far as Ceylon (AD 1510-15). During his first and second journeys he had visited various religious places and met people of different faiths. This explains why references to all major religious traditions of that time are found in his hymns, and shows what rich experiences he had gained by that time.

This dhundhūkārā hymn has sixteen long verses. In verse 1 Nānak refers to the pre-creation state and the Infinite Lord's state at that time. In verses 2 and 3 a general reference to the non-existent creation is given. Verses 4, 6, 7, 8, 10 and 13 (part) speak of the non-existence of various Hindu gods, religious practices, scriptures, etc. In the same way, verses 5 and 9 refer to the Sant and Nātha traditions, mentioning the non-existence of their leaders Gorakh and Machindra. In verses 11 and 13 (part) Nānak talks about the non-existence of the Muslim religious practices, scripture, etc., and in verse 12 again he speaks of the non-existence of general human relationships.

[7]I. Sunil Kumar Das, *Sri Caitanya and Guru Nānak,* Calcutta, 1985, pp. 124-5.
II. Anil Chandra Banerjee, *Guru Nānak and His Times,* Patiala, 1984, pp. 153-4.
III. Sher Singh, *Philosophy of Sikhism,* Amritsar, 1986, p. 180.
IV. Kohli, op. cit., pp. 80-1.
V. B.S. Khosla, *Guru Nānak's Conception of the Origin of the Universe in Guru Nānak: A Homage,* ed. K.R. Srivasa Iyengar, New Delhi, 1973, pp. 110-11.
VI. Wazir Singh, *The Sikh Cosmology in Journal of Sikh Studies,* vol. VI, no. 2, 2 August 1979, p. 73.

[8] Quoted in *A History of Indian Philosophy* by Surendranath Dasgupta, vol. 1, Delhi, 1988 (rpt.), p. 24.

[9] Maurice Phillips, *The Teaching of the Vedas,* Delhi, 1976 (rpt.), p. 114.

[10] Vīr Singh, 1926, p. 172.

In these first 13 verses Nānak makes two very important points: First, there was a state of non-existence of the world and all his negations refer to this very fact. Second, there existed the infinite, imperceptible and unseen (Lord or Being) and His will Hukamu (verse 1 and last part of verse 13). The overall stress here is on the absoluteness or absolute nature of the Creator.

In the second part of the dhundhūkārā hymn (verses 14, 15, 16) Nānak describes how the creation took place. He first of all makes clear the reason behind creation. It was because of the 'Will' (bhāṇā) of the Creator. Then in verses 14 (part) and 15, he describes how the Creator made this whole world, including the three main gods, Brahma, Vishnu and Shiva. In verse 16, Nānak says that he has received this knowledge through a Perfect Teacher.

The most important point, or the summary, of this hymn is found in the last part of verse 15: gupatahu paragatī āidā, 'from the unmanifest, He became manifest'. Through the act of creation the Creator Lord (who is absolute in His nature, but imperceptible and unseen) made Himself known. So here we find that through His bhāṇā, His 'Will' and in the ensuing act of creation, he has effected revelation of His nature through His created world.

The last point to be examined about the dhundhūkārā hymn is the phrase 'dhundhūkārā' itself. Three main translators have translated it as 'chaos' (Gopal Singh),[11] 'utter darkness' (Man Mohan Singh)[12] and 'darkness' (Talib).[13] We have translated it above as 'deep darkness'. In Punjabī the meaning of this phrase dhundhūkārā is 'darkness', and the meaning of its root dhund is 'mist'.[14] Therefore the literal meaning may be 'mistiness'. These renderings of course leave the question whether 'darkness' or 'mistiness' or even 'chaos' existed already, or whether it also was made. But one argument in favour of the concept of creation 'out of nothing' is based on this phrase and its meaning.[15]

But the important point which needs to be remembered is that through this phrase, dhundhūkārā, Nānak tried to describe the pre-

[11] Gopal Singh, vol. 4, p. 983.

[12] Man Mohan Singh, vol. 6, p. 3396.

[13] Talib, vol. 2, p. 2114.

[14] *Punjabī Kosha*, vol. III, pp. 510, 511.

[15] Maurice Phillips, p. 119.

creation state, the 'nothing' out of which the Creator made the creation. In the first part of the hymn, verses 1-13 Nānak described very clearly the non-existent state of creation in his negative references to this world. So the implied meaning of dhundhūkārā can be 'non-existence', because there was nothing. This point will be referred to again at a later stage, and we can leave the discussion at this point, in order to move to the next section on sunnu.

4.2.2.2. *Sunnu*

The second hymn quoted above in section 4.2.2.1. is called the Sunnu creation hymn. This hymn is also a long one, having 16 long verses extending over two pages of the *Ādi Granth* (pp. 1037, 1038). From the content as well as the main terms used in the hymn, and also after comparing it with the language and content of Nānak's other writings, particularly verses 50 and 51, of Sidh Gosat, it becomes clear that this hymn is addressed to a person or persons with a Buddhist background.[16] One such group, with whom Nānak is known to have come into contact, was the Sant (or nātha) religious group who shared the Buddhist religious outlook. According to G.S. Khosla, Nānak composed this hymn while having a dialogue with a Lama.[17]

This hymn does not present any views about the pre-creation state, except that in verse 1 Nānak speaks of the Absolute (aparampari) nature of the Creator, who is not only infinite (apārī), but also unique and different (nirālamu apara). The point which needs to be noted here is that He is not the same as his creation and is not identical with it. This is one impression one can get from the content of this hymn, particularly from verses like 'From the unattributed void they came into existence and in the same they will merge'. In verse 10 Nānak makes this point clear, 'the Absolute (aparampari) Lord Himself caused (Kāranu) it all'. Again the Creator's infinite and unique (apara nirālamu) nature is stressed. These thoughts of Nānak's make it very clear that his concept of creation is opposed to the Pantheistic view.

As was mentioned above, the list of created beings given in the sunnu hymn is very similar to that in the dhundhūkārā hymn, and

[16] *AG*, p. 943.

[17] Khosla, op. cit., p. 115.

therefore the general discussion of the content of this hymn does not need to be repeated. But the important point for discussion here is the word sunnu itself. Various translations of the *Ādi Granth* also create a problem about this word, because they do not agree about its meaning. For example, Gopal Singh has translated it as 'Absolute Self'[18] and very close to this is Man Mohan Singh's rendering 'the Absolute Lord'.[19] The most recent translation is that of Talib, who translated sunnu as 'Void'.[20] Our rendering is also close to Talib's.

As is well known, the concept Sunu (Void) or Sunyavada has a Buddhist background. Mahāyāna, one of the major sects of Buddhism, believed in it, and its thinker Nāgārjuna expounded it. This doctrine rejects all theories of causality, on the grounds that cause and effect are identical. According to them ". . . causal changes are just a transformation of a single underlying substance. . . . All empirical phenomena are insubstantial, because relative, but yet their inner nature can be said to be constituted by Voidness. Thus the world as seen from the standpoint of discursive reason and perception is unreal, and in its place one must substitute an apprehension of the Void. This Void, admittedly very thinly described, functions in the system as a sort of Absolute; thus the Void or Suchness (as it is sometimes referred to) is, in effect, the Ultimate Reality."[21]

On the basis of the above comment one can say without doubt that in the thought of Mahāyāna the Void is equal to the Absolute and that this concept has influenced most of the translators and commentators who translated sunnu as 'Absolute Lord or Self'. But once this view is accepted, then it affects the whole thought pattern of the translation or interpretation. For example, in the translation of Gopal Singh the account of creation begins with this phrase "Out of His Absolute Self came . . ." and a similar pattern appears in Man Mohan Singh's version: "From the Absolute Lord issued (or came). . . ." Here the concept of creation as emanation comes to the fore and with it the philosophy of Monism. But as we have

[18] Gopal Singh, vol. 4, p. 990.

[19] Man Mohan Singh, vol. 6, p. 2119.

[20] Talib, vol. 2, p. 2119.

[21] Ninian Smart, *Doctrine and Argument in Indian Philosophy,* London, 1964, 54-5.

already seen, Nānak made it very clear in verses 1 and 10 and also in 15, that the Creator is unique and separate, because He Himself is the cause of all that we see in this World. In fact, in verse 7 he used the term Karatai (Creator) saying "The Creator made and displayed the creation" (utabhuja). It will be seen in our later discussion, that the Void concept, which makes this world insubstantial and unreal, is not applicable to the views of Nānak.

4.2.2.3. *Aṇḍaja*

Unlike the first two creation hymns, dhundhūkārā and sunnu, there is less problem with the translation of this hymn, except that Man Mohan Singh has rendered aṇḍaja as 'spheres',[22] without much support. It seems that he has taken aṇḍaja's shape as round or circular, and so has translated it as sphere. But there is one other Panjābī word mandala which means sphere or circle.[23] Anyhow the meaning of aṇḍaja is very clear—born of the Egg and Nānak has used even the same word in another hymn, where he says:

> *Aṇḍaja jeraja utabhuja setaja tere kite jantā.*[24]
>
> Those who are born of egg, placenta, earth and sweat—all beings are your creation.

The authoritative Punjābī source gives the meaning of aṇḍaja as egg.[25]

The details of the created world given in this hymn again agree with the other two creation hymns. But this hymn is not an independent hymn; it is in fact part of a longer poem written by Nānak in Rāga Bilāvalu. Nānak used the 15 lunar days as a framework for the whole poem. On the first lunar day he gives a description of the Absolute Being, who according to him is: One, but unique (nirālā), eternal, without birth, without identity, without impurity inaccessible, inscrutable, without form, but pervading every human heart (see Chap. One, Sec. 1.3.1). Then after describing the Absolute nature of the Creator, on the second lunar day he describes the basic problems a human being faces, death, lust, etc.

[22] Man Mohan Singh, vol. 5, p. 2732.
[23] S.V., *Punjabī Kosa*, vol. 5, 'mandala', p. 66.
[24] *AG*, p. 596.
[25] S.V., Kahan Singh, 'Aṇḍaja', p. 113.

After all this, in the last part of the lunar day, and on the third and fourth days he narrates the creation story. (On the remaining lunar days 5-15, Nānak gave a number of other instructions.)

He began with the Creator's initiative in creation (āpe, Himself). The list of what is created, as in the other two hymns of Nānak, includes earth, sky, night, day, gods and goddesses, including Brahma, Vishnu, Shiva, lights, Vedas, Puranas, Shastras, etc. This hymn makes two points very clear (a) that the Creator not only made all, but also (b) that he takes care of all (vekhaṇhāru). Nānak lays special stress on the fact that there is only one Creator, whom he addresses on the first lunar day as ekaṁkāru, the One Absolute Being. The phrase he used, to say this is extremely powerful, avaru nā dūjā sirajaṇahāra: (of the creation) no other one (second) is Creator (except Him).

The problem in this hymn concerns the use of aṇḍaja (born of the Egg? the Egg?), if one takes the meaning of aṇḍaja phoṛi joṛi vichoṛi to be 'by breaking the Egg He joined and unjoined'. The implication of 'Egg' here is that the Creator is making His creation from pre-existing matter. The same question arose concerning dhundhūkārā (deep darkness) regarded as pre-existing, but in this hymn the act of creation is directly related to the 'Egg'. Also there is an echo of the well-known myth of creation from Hiraṇyagarbha, the golden womb.[26] According to this myth the Creator Lord first arose from a golden egg and then created all. According to Manu Hiraṇyagarbha is the name of Brahma, who took birth in the golden egg and for one year lived in this egg. While Brahma was still in the egg, according to his wish he broke the egg, of which one part became heaven and the other earth.[27]

But in a number of places in this work it has been pointed out that Nānak employed phrases and names to suit the context or the people he was with (see Chap. Two, Sec. 2.4.3). Also in the first two hymns we noted that they were addressed to different groups. This argument also applies here. Nānak used the symbol of aṇḍaja (Egg) to express his thoughts about the creation. Here, as we said above, his stress is on the One Lord as creator, and in this hymn he has also stressed that

[26] Phillips, op. cit., pp. 122-32.
[27] Kahan Singh, p. 276.

all gods and goddesses, including Brahma, Vishnu and Shiva, are part of the created world. In fact, the question of creation from pre-existing matter (Egg) was not considered in this hymn. Part of the reason for this might be that it is not an independent hymn, being part of a longer poem, in which many other basic thoughts and teachings were included. But the problem of pre-existing matter was clearly dealt with in Nānak's other hymns, especially in the first creation hymn which we have quoted, the dhundhūkārā.

4.3. MORE REFERENCES TO THE CREATOR AND CREATION

Before we conclude this chapter, it will be worth our while to examine some selected references concerning both the Creator and Creation in Nānak's other hymns. Some of these will throw further light on various aspects of Nānak's creation concept. For example, how, why and when was the creation created? Is this creation eternal or unreal? Who supports it or keeps it going? In this section we examine these questions.

4.3.1. How was Creation Created?

Nānak answers this question in Japu twice. He says:

> *Hukami hovani ākāru.*[28]
>
> By His order the creation (forms) came into being.

Again Nānak says:

> *Kitā pasāu Iko Kavāu.*[29]
>
> He made the world's expanse with one saying.

In Dakhaṇī Oṁkāru Nānak says:

> *Oṁkāri Brahama upati*[30]
>
> Oṁkāri produced (begot) Brahma.

The phrase, Oṁkāri, was discussed at length. In the second quotation from Japu given above, the significant word is 'kavāu' of which it was noted earlier that (like Oṁkāri) it is related to sabad (word) as agent of creation (1.4). In the first hymn, hukami also refers to the

[28] *AG*, p. 1.
[29] *AG*, p. 3.
[30] *AG*, p. 74.

same point, because an order is also given through the use of a word or words. Therefore the word is the agent, which the Creator used to make this world.

4.3.2. When was Creation Created?

Nānak raised this question in Japu. He says:

Kavaṇu su velā vakhatu
Kavaṇu Kavan thiti Kavaṇu varu.
Kavaṇi si rati māhu
Kavaṇu jitu hoā ākāru.[31]

What was the time or movement,
and what was the date or day,
What was the season or month,
when the creation was made, or when forms came into being?

In the same place in Japu, Nānak also gives the answer to this question. But before giving the answer he adds, Pandits cannot answer this question on the basis of their knowledge of Puranic texts, nor the Qāzis from the Qoran. Even the Nātha Yogī cannot tell the day, season or month, when the creation was made. Nānak's answer is:

Jā Karatā sirathi Ku sāje
Āpe jānai soi.[32]

The Creator who fashioned the creation,
He only knows the time (of creation).

4.3.3. Why was Creation Created ?

Nānak's answer to this question is as follows:

Guramukhi dharatī sāja.[33]

It is for the saints He has fashioned this earth. In another place Nānak says:

Dharati upāiādhari dharamasālā.[34]

[31] *AG*, p. 7.
[32] *AG*, p. 7.
[33] *AG*, p. 941
[34] *AG*, p. 1033.

He made this earth as place of practising righteousness.

Nānak also said that human beings are created to serve the Creator:

Phuramanī hai Kar Khasamī padathāiā.[35]

The master has sent the human being into this world with an order to serve Him.

So one of the purposes of this world is that the Creator wants human beings to live in it and practice righteousness. This thought is expressed in the Aṇḍaja hymn also: baisaṇa Ku thāu (places to live).

4.3.4. Is this Creation Ureal?

Nānak says:

Nānak sace ki sācī Kāra,[36] .

O Nānak, True is creation of the True One.

In Vār Āsā Nānak again says:

Sace tere Khand sace brahamandu;
Sace tere loa sace ākār.[37]

True are your continents and true are your firmaments,
True are your worlds and true are your creation (forms).

These references do not need any explanation because they are self-explanatory. Everything the Creator has created is real and true.

4.3.5. Is this Creation Eternal?

Ḍhāhi usāre dhare dhiānu.[38]

He destroys, makes, holds and gives thoughts.

The above reference makes it clear that this creation is not eternal. The Creator created it many times and also destroyed it. There are a number of hymns, where Nānak makes it clear that except the Creator Himself, nothing in this world is eternal. For example:

[35] *AG*, p. 142.
[36] *AG*, p. 7.
[37] *AG*, p. 463.
[38] *AG*, p. 354.

i. *Aasathiru Karatā dekhiaī horu Ketī avai jai.*[39]

The Creator is the only one seen as stable,
all others continue coming and going.

ii. *Sabha duni avanu jāvani mukāmu*
Iku rahīmu.[40]

The whole world is subject to coming and going,
Only the merciful Lord is permanent.

4.3.6. What is the Extent of the Creation ?

In Rāga Āsā Nānak raised the question of the extent of the creation in these words:

Nāli Kuṭambu sathi varadātā Brahama bhalaṇ sirasti gaiā.
Āgai antu na paio.[41]

Brahma the giver of boons with his family members
went to find (the extent) of the creation;
but even going further and further, he could not find the end.

In Japu Nānak gives his views about the extent of the creation:

Anta na jāpai pārā vāru.[42]

It seems there is no limit of His created creation.

This is because it is equal to the Name of the Creator, about which Nānak says:

Jetā Kitā tetā nāu.[43]

As Your creation is great, so is your Name.

4.3.7. Who Takes Care of the Creation?

In a number of hymns Nānak says that the Creator Himself provides for the needs and takes care of His Creation. Examples:

i. *Nānak jant upāi Kai samūle sabhanaha.*[44]

[39] *AG*, p. 54.
[40] *AG*, p. 64.
[41] *AG*, p. 350.
[42] *AG*, p. 5.
[43] *AG*, p. 5.
[44] *AG*, p. 466.

O Nānak, after making all the beings,
He Himself takes care of them all.

ii. *So Karatā Kādar Karīmu de*
jīāi rijak samabāhi[45]

The Creator, who is almighty and gracious, gives food to all.

iii. *Āpe Satigaru āpe savaku*
āpe sirasti upāi he.[46]

He Himself the True Gurū, Himself the Servant, He Himself made the creation.

4.4. CONCLUDING REMARKS

From the discussion in this chapter of various creation hymns and other references, two aspects of the nature of the Creator (who is Ik Oṁkār), become clear, namely, the Absolute (unmanifested) and the Personal (mainfested). These two are summed up in the phrase of dhundhūkārā hymn, gupatahu paragatī āidā (from the unmanifest, He becomes manifest). The same thought is also found in the sunnu hymn, sunnu upajī ('from the unattributed Void they came into existence'). The Aṇḍaja hymn affirms the personal aspect of sirajaṇahārā, the Creator. The three key phrases dhundhūkārā, sunnu and aṇḍaja refer to the pre-creation state.

The question of creation coming out of 'nothing', or 'pre-existent matter', or 'out of the Creator', is not the basic subject of Nānak's creation hymns. His basic subject is the sovereignty of the Creator over His creation. At the same time he maintains the distinction between the Creator and creation. Phrases like nirālamu (different), apāra (separate), nirālā (unique), etc., are pointers to this fact. The quotations in Sec. 4.3 under the head 'More References to the Creator and creation' again establish the fact of the Creator's lordship and eternity. Also the Personal aspect of the Creator's nature becomes further evident in this Section (4.3.7), to which phrases like samūle (takes care) and de . . . rijak (gives food) are pointers.

[45] *AG*, p. 474.
[46] *AG*, p. 1026.

CHAPTER FIVE

Gurparasādi

5.1. INTRODUCTION

It may be good to begin this chapter by referring to the Basic Credal Statement of the religion of Nānak, Mūl Mantr, in which Ik Oṁkār occurs 568 times, and Sati and also the gurparasādi 567 times.[1] In chapter One, we discussed the first unit of this Statement, Ik Oṁkār, which is the core of Nānak's basic doctrine. In chapter Two, the second unit, satinãmu, was studied in detail. In chapter Three, we examined the basic attributes of Ik Oṁkār, which are listed in the basic Credal Statement, karatā purakhu, nirabhaü niraviru, akāla mūrati and ajūnī saiṁbhaṁ. Chapter Four contained an analysis of one of the most important attributes of Ik Oṁkār—Karatā. In all these chapters one of the points which has become clear is that one of Nānak's main concerns in all his hymns was to share with others his experience of Ik Oṁkār or the Ultimate Reality, whom he addressed with many names and who has many attributes. Through these many names and attributes he has indicated the two aspects of the nature of Ik Oṁkār, the Absolute and the Personal. But though we have referred several times in the earlier chapters to the question how a human being can know or perceive these two aspects of Ik Oṁkār, this important issue has not so far been dicussed systematically.

At the end of the Mūl Mantr, Nānak himself dealt with this issue by adding the last unit, gurparasādi,[2] which is the key to the revelation of Ik Oṁkār, and in this chapter this will be the subject of our study. Different translators and commentators give different renderings of this important expression, and, therefore, it will be good to begin this discussion by looking at these.

[1] Cf. Introd. note 35, p. 21.

[2] Vide, Prologue, p. 23.

5.2. GURPARASĀDI

A number of translators have made an attempt to translate this important phrase, some of which are given here:

Trumpp: By the favour of the Gurū.[3]
Macauliffe: By the favour of the Gurū.[4]
Gopal Singh: By the Grace of One Supreme Being. . . . The Enlightener.[5]
Man Mohan Singh: By the Gurū's grace (he is obtained).[6]
Talib: Realized by the grace of the Holy Preceptor.[7]

Besides the above five major English translations of the *Ādi Granth,* the following renderings are taken from some translations restricted to Japu, the first book of the *Ādi Granth:*

Teja Singh: By the grace of the One Supreme Being . . . the Enlightener.[8]
Puran Singh: Through the Grace of His true servant, continually repeat His name.[9]
Dewan Singh: He is known and realised by the grace of the Gurū.[10]
Khushwant Singh: By His grace shalt thou worship Him.[11]
Doabia: He is realised by the kindness of the true Gurū.[12]

[3] Trumpp, p. 1.
[4] Macauliffe, vol. I, p. 95.
[5] Gopal Singh, vol. I, p. 1.
[6] Man Mohan Singh, vol. I, p. 1.
[7] Talib, vol. I, p. 1.
[8] Teja Singh (trans.), *The Japuji,* Amritsar, 7th edn. 1974, p. 19.
[9] Puran Singh (trans.), 'Japuji Sahib', in *Gurū Nānak and His Japuji,* by Parkash Singh, Amritsar, 1969, p. 64.
[10] Dewan Singh (trans.), *Gurū Nānak's Message in Japuji,* Amritsar, 1970, p. 81.
[11] Khushwant Singh (trans.), 'Japuji—The Morning Prayer', in *A History of the Sikhs,* vol. 1: *1469-1839* by Khushwant Singh, Delhi, Indian Edition, 1977, p. 324.
[12] Harbans Singh Doabia (trans.), *'Jap(u) Ji' Sacred Nit Nem,* Amritsar, 1985 (rpt.), p. 2.

There are a number of commentators, both in English and Punjābī, who share one or other of the above views. Here only four of these—three who have commented in Panjābī and one in Hindi are quoted:

Sāhib Singh: 'Ik Oṁkār Gurū de parasāda nāla,'meaning 'with the grace of Gurū Ik Oṁkāru is known'.[13]

Vīr Singh: Gurū dē Kirapā nāla' meaning 'with the favour of Gurū'.[14]

Jodh Singh: 'Paramātamā dā japa Gurū dī parsanatā dā pātara ho ke kara,' meaning 'Being in the happiness of Gurū you should meditate on Supreme Soul (God)'.[15]

Vinoba Bhave: 'Bhagavāna ki kripā se', meaning 'By the favour of God.'[16]

One of the most recent translations of Japu is in German, by Monika Thiel-Horstmann, who translated gurparasādi as follows:

Durch des Gurus Gnade wird Er erkannt.[17]

Through the Gurū's grace he is known.

The above translators and commentators can be divided into four groups on the basis of their translations and interpretations:

i. The first group includes Trumpp, Macauliffe, Man Mohan Singh, Dewan Singh, Doabia, Sāhib Singh, Vīr Singh, Vinoba Bhave and Monika Thiel-Horstmann. These translators have given an over-simplified rendering of gurparasādi, 'by the favour or grace of the Gurū'; but Man Mohan Singh, Talib, Dewan Singh, Doabia and Sāhib Singh have added a qualifying phrase, that Ik Oaṁkār is known or realized by the grace of the Gurū.

ii. The second group includes Gopal Singh and Teja Singh. These two translators have taken gurparasādi as two

[13] Sahib Singh (Tīkākāra), p. 47.
[14] Vīr Singh, 1981, p. 32.
[15] Bhāī Jodh Singh, *Japuji Satika* (Panjābī), Patiala, 1980, p. 2.
[16] Vinoba Bhave, *Japuji* (Hindi commentary), Varanasi, 2nd edn., April 1965, p. 35.
[17] Monika Thiel-Horstmann, *Leben Aus Der Wahrheit*, Zurich, 1988, p. 35.

separate terms, gur and parasādi (unlike the first group which has taken gurparasādi as one unit) in their rendering. Gopal Singh has himself explained how he arrived at his meaning. He outright rejects the view of the first group, because according to him they have wrongly joined the word gur to parasādi and have given the meaning "By favour (or grace) of the Gurū. . . . " He says "But here Gurū Nānak is giving in monosyllables the attributes of God. The Gurū, therefore, is Gurū-in-God whose Grace is invoked. As such 'Gurū' can only be rendered as 'Enlightener', which is also its literal meaning in Sanskrit."[18]

iii. In the third group are Talib and Puran Singh, whose renderings indicate that they refer to a Gurū other than Ik Oṁkār. Talib has rendered gura as 'the Holy Preceptor' and Puran Singh as 'His true servant'. In the case of Puran Singh it is clear that he has taken the meaning of gura as understood by an average Sikh believer today, which refers either to Nānak or to all the Ten Gurūs. Talib's reason is found in his explanation of the meaning of gura parasādi in the introduction to his translation and also in his other major work 'Guru Nanak: His Personality and Vision'. He says: 'Gurparasadi . . . the realization of the Supreme Being comes by the grace of Preceptor, the holy Gurū.'[19] In this explanation the implication of self-revelation by Ik Oṁkār (the Supreme Being) has been set aside. In the other work mentioned above Talib said: "While literally, this word may be rendered as Teacher, Guide, Preceptor, its further connotations are wide. Gurū stands in Sikh religious thought as much for the human Teacher or Preceptor as for the Divine. In the Scripture Sat-Gurū (Eternal Teacher or Guide) usually stands for God."[20] Again it is clear that Talib in his rendering of gurparasādi is more concerned with the human Gurū than with Ik Oṁkār. In fact, by giving in a

[18] Gopal Singh, vol. 1, p. 32 (fn.).
[19] Talib, Introduction, p. xlvi.
[20] Gurbachan Singh Talib, *Gurū Nānak: His Personality and Vision*, Delhi, 1969, p. 141.

footnote an alternative rendering, 'Realised through Divine grace' he has strengthened his argument.

iv. In the last and fourth group are Puran Singh and Khushwant Singh, who connect 'gurparasādi' with the word 'Japu'. This word actually is the title of the work Japu, which immediately follows after Mūl Mantr. But the Mūl Mantr and Japu are two different works written during different periods.[21] But Puran Singh and Khushwant Singh have run the two together in their renderings: 'through the grace of His true Servant, continually repeat His name' and 'By His grace shalt thou worship Him. In these two renderings all stress on the revelation or realization aspect of Ik Oṁkār is lost.

We have already seen how some translators have understood gura parasādi. We have also said in our introductory remarks that with gura parasādi, Nānak added a new subject to the Mūl Mantr, and that by adding this phrase Nānak made provision for the knowledge of Ik Oṁkār, who otherwise is formless, unknown, unseen, invisible, inaccessible, imperceptible, etc. (see Chap. One Sec.1.3.1). With this view, almost all the above translators agree to some extent, except Puran Singh and Khushwant Singh (the fourth group). The position of the translators belonging to the second group is also different in so far as they have taken gurparasādi as two separate terms and have translated them as two attributes of Ik Oṁkār. Gopal Singh made his position clear in his explanation which was quoted above. There are other scholars also who agree with this group. The clear-est example is Taran Singh, who very strongly advocated this position.[22] But this view is influenced by the later development of gurūship after Nānak, which has been summarized very nicely by W. Owen Cole in his work 'The Gurū in Sikhism'.[23] The same problem has been faced by the translators belonging to the third

[21] Vide, Lal Singh, "Introduction", *Hymns of Gurū Nānak*, Language Department, Punjab, Patiala, 1972, pp. III and IX.

[22] Taran Singh, "The Nature of Guruship in the Guru Granth", *The Nature of Guruship*, ed. C. O'McMullen, Delhi, 1976, p. 26.

[23] W. Owen Cole, *The Gurū in Sikhism*, London, 1982, pp. 29-38.

group who apparently laid more stress on the human aspect of the Gurū. The translators of the first group, who rendered gurparasādi as 'By the favour or grace of Gurū', seem to be correct, but their way of putting it suggests that they have over-simplified the whole concept or concepts. It is, therefore, vital for the present work to examine the meaning and implications of gurparasādi and to see what Nānak meant by this phrase. For convenience, the two words, gur and parasādi, will be taken separately in the next two sections, and then in the following section they will be taken together as one phrase.

5.3. GUR

There are a number of questions to be considered in connection with the concept of gur: the meaning of the term gur, the place of gur in the Mūl Mantr, who is gur, how to meet gur, the role of gur, etc. These questions are discussed here in turn.

5.3.1. The Meaning of the Term Gur

There are a number of possible derivations of the term gur on the basis of which various interpretations are given. Two of these are worth mentioning here, as they are close to the sense expressed in the hymns of Nānak. According to one derivation, gur is made up of two roots, 'gu' meaning 'darkness' and 'ru' meaning 'remover'. So gur is one who removes darkness or ignorance or false conceptions.[24] According to the second derivation the Sanskrit root of the noun gur or Gurū is gri, which means 'to swallow' or 'to make understand'. So the Gurū is one who swallows or eats up ignorance and makes one understand the real wisdom.[25]

5.3.2. The Place of Gur in the Mūl Mantr

In the Introduction, note 35 (p. 21) mention has already been made of the five different forms of the Mūl Mantr, including shorter and longer ones. These five forms occur 568 times in the *Ādi Granth*, of which the following shorter form occurs 524 times:

[24] Hardev Bhari, 'A Linguistic Analysis of the Mul Mantr', *Sikh Concept of the Divine*, ed. Pritam Singh, Amritsar, 1985, p. 159.
[25] Kahan Singh, p. 415.

Ik Oṁkār satigurparasādi.[26]

The important point to note here is that in the above form gura is joined with sati as one phrase. But in the remaining forms (except for the one in which "Ik Oṁkār" occurs by itself),[27] gura is joined with parasādi, gurparasādi.[28] Some related points will become clear when the hymns of Nānak are examined, but here the point should be made that the form satigura may have come in at the time of the compilation of the *Ādi Granth,* because by that time 'Satigura' was in common use. This can be seen in the vārs of Bhāī Gurdās.[29]

However, as far as we are concerned, the complete text of the Mūl Mantr is the one which gives the right sequence of the phrases and terms used by Nānak, and therefore gurparasādi is the correct expression for consideration here.

5.3.3. Who is the Gur?

One of the fundamental questions related to Nānak's concept of the Gurū has always been: Who is the Gurū, about whom he speaks in his hymns? Does he have in mind any human Gurū? If not, then whom does he address as Gur or Satigurū? In view of certain similarities between his teaching and that of Kabīr, some early writers like J.N. Farquhar tried to show that Nānak was Kabīr's disciple.[30] A full discussion of this issue can again be found in W. Owen Cole's work on 'The Gurū in Sikhism'.[31] But the question about Nānak's Gurū is not new, and was raised even during his lifetime. This happened when he held discussions with the Siddās and Yogīs, who asked him:

[26] *AG,* pp. 8, 10, 12, 14, 26, 53, 64, 71, 74, 78, 79, etc.
[27] *AG,* p. 1353.
[28] *AG,* pp. 1, 94, 151, 347, 462, 475, 489, 527, 537, 595, 660, 711, 721, 728, 795, 859, 876, 975, 984, 989, 1125, 1168, 1197, 1254, 1294, 1319, 1327, 1352, 1353, 1353 (second time), 1385, and 1910.
Note: On page 462, 475, 1353 Gur and Parasādi have been printed separately in the Edition of the *Ādi Srī Granth Sāhib Ji, Srī Damadamī Bīr, Panā,* Parakasāk Bhāī Jawahar Singh Kirpāl Singh and Lampanī, Amritsar, N.d.
[29] Gurdās, 1:17, 27; 3:1, 7, 12, 20; 5.13; 6.1, 19; 7.18; 9.10; 10.19; 11.1, 26, etc.
[30] J.N. Farquhar, 'A Primer of Hinduism', London, 1911, p. 124.
[31] W. Owen Cole, op. cit., pp. 8-11.

Tera Kavaṇu Gurū jis kātu celā.[32]

Who is your Gurū, of whom you are the disciple?

Nānak replied:

Sabadu Gurū surati dhuni celā. . .
Nānak jugi jugi gura Gopālā.[33]

The Word is my Gurū, my inner being (mind), which meditates continually, is the disciple . . .

The Gurū of Nānak throughout the ages is the Gopālā. So Nānak's Gurū is the Word, as well as Ik Oṁkāru himself, whom he addresses as Gopālā, the Cherisher of the world.[34]

In a number of other hymns Nānak expresses the same view that Ik Oṁkāru, or the Lord Himself, is the Gurū, for whom he has different names:

i. . . . *amru so guru karatāru.*[35]

. . . Only that Gurū Creator is eternal.

ii. *Gurū Parmasaru Nānak bhetio sācai sabadi niberā.*[36]

Nānak has met the Gurū—the Supreme Lord—and the true Word is salvation.

iii. *Satigurū purakhu data vad dāṇā.*[37]

Satigurū, the Being, is the provider and all-wise.

iv. *Hari gura pūre kī ota parātī.*[38]

I have come under the protection of the perfect Lord Gurū.

v. *Gurū devā gura alakha abhevā tirbhavan sojhi gura ki sevā.*
Āpe dāte karī gure dātai pāiā alakha abhevā.[39]

The Divine (Devā) Gurū is that Gurū, who is unseen and beyond understanding.

[32] *AG*, p. 941.
[33] AG, p. 942.
[34] Cf. post Clarence Osmond Mcmullen, 'Religious Beliefs and Practices of the Sikhs in Rural Punjab', New Delhi, 1989, p. 56.
[35] *AG*, p. 63.
[36] *AG*, p. 977.
[37] *AG*, p. 1030.
[38] *AG*, p. 1031.
[39] *AG*, p. 1125.

Through the service of the Gurū one gets the knowledge of the three worlds.
The Giver, the Gurū himself, has given the gift, and I have met the unseen and incomprehensible (Lord).

The above hymns do not need much comment, because all agree on one point, concerning the identity of Nānak's Gurū with Kartāru (the Creator), Paramasaru (the Supreme Lord), Purakhu (the Being), Hari (Lord), Pūre (the Perfect), Devā (the Divine), etc. All these titles recall the discussions which took place on the various names of the Ik Oṁkār in Chapter Two (2.4.3).

Besides declaring that Ik Oṁkār Himself his Gurū, Nānak also stresses the Oneness of the Gurū. There may be human gurūs, but even these are all One (implied meaning: Ik Oṁkār):

Chia ghar chia gura chia opadessa,
Gura Gurū eko vesa anek.[40]

There are six systems, six teachers and six doctors.
But the Gurū, of gurūs is the One who has many forms.

Nānak also addreses the things of Nature as Gurū. Here again we find the all-pervading (omnipresent) aspect of Ik Oaṁkār, and Nānak sees this presence as Gurū, Father and Mother. He says in the closing sloka of Japu:

Pavaṇu Gurū pāṇī pita mātā dharti . . .[41]

Air is Gurū, the Father is water, the Mother is earth . . .

Besides affirming who was his Gurū, Nānak also testifies that he always received his message directly from the Lord. He says:

Jaioi mai āvai khasama ki baṇī taiṛa
Karī giānu ve Lalo.[42]

As the Word of the Lord comes to me,
The same I let others know, O Lālo.

5.3.4. How does One Meet the Gur?

In a number of hymns Nānak explains how one can meet Gur or Satigurū. For example:

[40] *AG*, p. 12, 357.
[41] *AG*, p. 8.
[42] *AG*, p. 722.

i. *Nadari kare tā satigurū milai.*[43]

If the Lord looks with His merciful glance, then one meets satigurū.

ii. *Āpe bakhase satigurū milai.*[44]

(The Lord) Himself forgives and He Himself arranges (for a person) to meet Satigurū.

Both these hymns make it clear that it is only through the grace of the Lord that one can meet the True Teacher. In another hymn Nānak explains that one who gets imbued with the Truth meets the Gurū.

Saci rate gura meliai,
Sace saci samāi.[45]

Being imbued with the Truth, one meets the Gurū;
one who is true gets absorbed in the Truth (Lord).

5.3.5. The Role of the Gur

Among the Indian religious traditions it is perhaps Nānak who gave the highest place to the role of the Gurū or a Gurū. This one can see when Nānak states the essence of Sikhism in relation to the role of the Gurū in the following hymn:

Sikhi sikhiā Gura vīcāre.
Nadarī Karamī laghāe pāre.[46]

The education of discipleship is to meditate upon the Gura.
Through His grace He takes one across.

Here the term 'Sikhi' needs to be noted, because today this is synonymous with the Sikh religion or Sikhism.[47] According to Nānak, the Formless One, who is Ik Oṁkār or Brahamu, has placed Himself in the Gura or Satigurū, and it is only through the Gur that one can meet Ik Oṁkār. Nānak stated both these truths in the following hymn:

Binu satigura kinai na paio,
Binu satigura kinai na paio.

43 *AG*, p. 354.
44 *AG*, P. 415.
45 *AG*, p. 22.
46 *AG*, p. 465.
47 Kahan Singh, pp. 192-3.

Satigura vici āpu rakhionu,
Kari paragatu ākani suṇāiā.[48]

Without the true Gurū no one has attained Him,
Without the true Gurū no one has attained Him.
In the true Gurū He has placed Himself.
This I revealed openly by declaring it.

In a number of hymns Nānak says that the revelation of Ik Oṁkār or the knowledge of His presence is only possible through the favour of the Gurū. For example he says:

Gura kirapā te bājhīai sabhu Brahamu samāiā.[49]

Through the favour of the Gurū, one knows that
Brahamu is present in all.

Here we see Nānak saying the same thing as he said in the Mūl Mantr when using the phrase gurparasādi, which means that the knowledge of Ik Oṁkār or Brahamu is the Gurū's free gift or is given through the grace of the Gurū. There are a number of other references in Nānak's hymns, which state the same point. Here is one example:

Kahu Nānak guri Brahamu dikhāiā.[50]

The Gurū has shown the transcendent Lord (Brahamu),
says Nānak.

In Chapter One (1.3.1) reference has already been made to one of the famous hymns of Nānak which begins with ekama ekaṁkāru nirālā (One Absolute Being is unique). This hymn also mentions the attributes of his niraguṇa nature. In the same hymn Nānak says:

Gura kai sabadi mahalu gharu dīsai.[51]

Through the Gurū's Word (sabad) His living-place is seen in one's own house.

The close mystic relationship between the One and all beings is also seen because of satigurū. Nānak says of this:

[48] *AG*, p. 466.
[49] *AG*, p. 229.
[50] *AG*, p. 152.
[51] *AG*, p. 839.

Eka mahi sarab
Sarab mahi Eka,
Eha satigure dethi dīkhāī.[52]

All in One and One in all,
This vision satigurū has shown to me.

Again the unique One, who is above the limitation of birth (ajonī) and is self-born (sambhaü), is attained through the satigurū. Nānak says:

Āpi atītu ajonī sambhaü
Nānak Guramati so pāiā.[53]

He Himself is detached, above birth and self-born,
but He is attained through the teaching of the Gurū, O Nānak.

This hymn again refers to the experience of Ik Oṁkār's presence. In one of his discourses with yogis Nānak tells them that through the Gurū's instructions one can easily meet the Invisible Reality, who is pure in nature, and can also have communion with Him:

Gura bacanī avigate samāiāi
Tatu Nirañjanu sahaji lahai.[54]

Through the instructions of the Gurū, one can easily have communion with the Invisible Pure Reality and can also attain Him.

Mention should be made here that there are other concepts which are directly related to the knowledge of Ik Oṁkār or His revelation: nāmu, sabada, hukama, sacu, nadara, etc. In one of the hymns in Rāga Gauṛī, Nānak has brought together all these concepts.[55] We have already in Chapter Two examined in detail nāmu and sacu (2.2, 2.3, 2.3.1, 2.3.2). Mention has already been made above of nadara and it will be discussed in more detail in the next section. As regards hukama, sabada, and sacu, these are closely related to the concept of the gura. Examples which show this are:

52 *AG,* p. 907.
53 *AG,* p. 1042.
54 *AG,* p. 940.
55 *AG,* pp. 220-1.

i. *Gura ke sabadi hukamu pachāṇu*[56]

Through the Word of the Gurū His order is recognised.

ii. *Gura purai sacu samāiā.*[57]

Through the Perfect Gurū I am absorbed in Truth.

The best example to show the relationship of the above concepts to the role of the Gur can be found in the following hymn of Nānak:

Sākata nari sabadi sūrati kio pāiāi.
Sabad surati binu aīai jāiāi.
Nānak guramūkhi mukati parāinu
Hari purai bhāgi milaia
Nirabhaü satigurū hai rakhavālā.
Bhagati prāpati gura Gopālā . . .
gura sabadi nirañjanu pāiā . . .
Api atitu ajonī sambaü Nānak Gurumati so pāiā.
Anatar ki gati satigurū janai.
So Nirabhaü gura sabadi pachanai . . .
Nirabhaü so abh anatari vasia.
Ashinisi nāmi nirañjan rasiā . . .
Ūpari adi sarab tihu loi sacu
Nānak ammrita rasu pāiā.[58]

How can a worldly person gain awareness by the Word?
Without awareness of the Word transmigration continues.
With the support of the Gura one obtains salvation.
By perfect luck One meets the Lord.
The Satigura, the fearless One, is the watchkeeper, said Nānak.
From the Gura, the Cherisher, one receives the (gift of) loving devotion . . .
Through the Word of the Gura the Holy One is obtained . . .
He Himself is detached, above the limitation of natural birth and is self-born,
Nānak, He is obtained through the wisdom of the Gura.
only Satigura knows the inner state of (a human being).

56 *AG*, p. 223 (also see *AG*, p. 636).
57 *AG*, p. 879.
58 *AG*, p. 1042.

> One who recognizes the Word of Gura, becomes free from fear . . .
> In him the Fearless One lives,
> Who day and night is absorbed in the Name of the Holy One . . .
> He is the One, O Nānak, who receives the eternal joyful ammrita (nectar) from the Primal True (Word) Who is above all the three worlds.

Once again Nānak raised the basic question, which he has raised in the Japu: "How can one be true . . . ?(1.3). In Japu Nānak's answer is by keeping the hukama which one recognizes through the Word of the Gur (see the hymn quoted above). Here the question is repeated in a different form, 'How can a worldly person gain awareness by the Word?'Gur or Satigura is the key to the answer to the above basic question. The Gur knows the inner thoughts of humanity, and it is through his wisdom and support that one becomes aware of the Sabad (Word), and this one can get by being absorbed in the Name. At the end of this hymn, Nānak says that whoever does that, ultimately receives 'the eternal joyful ammrita from the Primal True Word'. Here 'ammrita rasu' is difficult to translate. The phrase hints at the mystic experience of the human being, which he or she receives through the Gur.

5.4. PARASĀDI

Along with Parasādi, we will consider in this section some other terms, which Nānak used in his hymns to express related ideas. These are nadara, karama, kirapā and diā. There are two other terms, rajā and bhāṇā, which also need consideration in order to understand Nānak's concept of Grace. Parasādi needs separate treatment, because of its special place in the Mūl Mantr. So the first set is considered first.

5.4.1. NADARA, KARAMA, KIRAPĀ AND DIĀ

The first two terms nadara and karama have Arabic roots. The literal meaning of nazara is 'seeing' or 'looking'. In Panjābī it has a number of meanings based on the root meaning—sight, glance, care, examination, mercy, favour, thinking, opinion, etc.[59] Nānak uses nadara, in various hymns, in which it has different meanings.

[59] S.V., *Punjābī Kosha,* vol. 3, p. 558.

Examples:

i. . . . *Nadarī mokhu duarū.*[60]

His mercy is the door of release.

ii. *Nānak nadarī nadarī nihāla,*[61]

Nānak, the Merciful (Lord) makes them happy with His favourable glance.

In the first hymn nadarī is used as a masculine noun, and is translated 'His mercy', it can also be rendered 'Merciful Lord'. In the second hymn nadarī occurs twice, and its second occurrence (which is rendered 'favourable glance') emphasizes the quality of the first and makes the concern of the Lord more concrete.

According to Nānak the 'One' who cannot be described in words (indescribable), can be beheld if He Himself looks with favour:

Nadarī Kare tā akhī vekhā kahaṇā kathanu na jāī.[62]

If He Himself looks with favour, then I can see Him with my eyes,
Otherwise He is both ineffable and indescribable.

The second term karami is not only connected with an Arabic root, Karama (as already mentioned), but it also has a Sanskrit root, Karama. If we take the first (Arabic) root, then the meaning is 'mercy' or 'favour'; and if we take the second (Sanskrit), then the meaning is 'work' or 'deed' or 'action'.[63] Nānak uses Karami with both these meanings in his hymns:

i. *Karami milai sacu . . .*[64]

Through His favour he unites a person with the True One.

ii. *Krami avai kapaṛā . . .*[65]

Through actions one attains birth (robe).

According to Nānak it is through the Merciful Lord's mercy that the separation between Him and human beings can be removed.

[60] *AG*, p. 2.
[61] *AG*, p. 8.
[62] *AG*, p. 596.
[63] Kahan Singh, p. 304.
[64] *AG*, p. 62.
[65] *AG*, p. 2.

Nānak nadarī karamu hoi javhi sagala Vijog.[66]

O Nānak, It is through the Mercy of the Merciful (Lord) that all separations are removed.

Kirapā is the third term which Nānak uses in his hymns to explain how Sāhib, the Lord, is related to human beings. For example he says:

Sāhibu hoi dialu kirapā kāre ta sai kara karāisī.[67]

If the Lord shows his compassion and bestows his mercy, then one can render Him service.

Kirapā is the Punjābī form of the Sanskrit word kṛpā. The root of kṛpā is kṛp, which means 'to pity'. On the basis of this root the following possible meanings of this expression are found in 'pity', 'tenderness', 'compassion',[68] Nānak also uses Kirapā with this meaning. One example has just been given. There are a number of hymns in which Nānak used Kirapā as the means of Lord's revelation. In the first example below Nānak uses the simile of a bridegroom for the Lord, who because of His compassion has come to marry His bride, who can be any human being:

Kari Kirapā apansi ghari śiā ta mili
sakhiā kāju racāiā.
Khelu dekhi mani anadu bhiā shu vīāhan āiā.[69]

When, because of His compassion, He came to His own home, then my female companions arranged for the marriage.
Seeing this play, my mind became joyful, because my bridegroom has come to marry me.

In another hymn Nānak first tells how the One Lord pervadeṣ everything, and then how the same Lord reveals Himself through his mercy:

Sabha mahi varata eko si.
Jis no kirapā kare tisu paragathu hoi.[70]

The One (Lord) pervades all;

66 *AG*, p. 954.
67 *AG*, p. 471.
68 V.S., Monier-Williams, p. 305.
69 *AG*, p. 351.
70 *AG*, p. 931.

to whomsoever He shows His mercy,
he reveals Himself.

Diā is another term, which Nānak uses in his hymns.[71] In Sanskrit this word means 'sympathy', 'compassion', 'pity for', etc.[72] An examples from Nānak's hymns is:

Praṇavati Nānak dāsni dāsā diā karahu diālā.[73]

Nānak, the slave of your slaves, prays before you,
O my merciful Lord have pity upon me.

5.4.2. RAJĀ, BHĀṆĀ

Along with rajā and bhāṇā there is a third term which can be considered here, namely, Hukama. Very few scholars have dealt with these terms, particularly bhāṇā. Among those who have studied these terms, McLeod is perhaps the first scholar who has made even a passing mention of bhāṇā. While discussing the concept of nadara and its rendering as 'grace', McLeod said that the English term 'grace' can mislead if used to translate Nānak's term nadara. However he did not develop his argument, except to say that bhāṇā is the only possible word which can mean 'favour'.[74] Following McLeod, three other scholars discussed this issue. Like McLeod Talib made a passing reference to rajā as well as to Bhāṇā in his discussion of the concept of hukama. He gives the meaning of hukama as Order or Command, and according to him it has also acquired the connotation of power, because of its use by Muslim rulers in India. According to Talib, both bhāṇā (desire, will) and rajā (will, volition) are equivalent to the concept of hukama. Hukama and Rajā he said come from an Arabic background, while bhāṇā comes from local Panjābī.[75] Grewal also referred to both bhāṇā and rajā, which according to him are almost synonymous with the word Hukama.[76] The fourth scholar who has discussed rajā and bhāṇā in

[71] *AG*, p. 149, 1022, 1113, 1171.
[72] V.S., Monier-William, p. 469.
[73] *AG*, p. 1171.
[74] W.H. Mcleod, *Gurū Nānak and the Sikh Religion*, Delhi, 1968, p. 206.
[75] Talib, Gurbachan Singh, op. cit., p. 144.
[76] J.S. Grewal, *Gurū Nānak in History*, Chandigarh, December 1969 (rpt. February 1979), p. 246.

more detail is Sardul Singh Kaveeshar, who writes in Panjābī. According to him the final goal of a human being is to gain union with the Supreme Soul (Param-Ātamā). The way to do this is by accepting the bhāṇā of the Akāla Purakh, by which he means accepting without any doubt the hukama of Paramātamā, which pervades the whole world. He further adds that this kind of life is known in Sikhism as rajā.[77] So according to him all these phrases—hukama, bhāṇā and rajā—are closely related both in meaning and use.

The first thing we learn from the above four scholars is the importance of bhāṇā, because whether one talks about hukama or about rajā, bhāṇā comes in on both sides. In Nānak's hymns also the concept of bhāṇā is used in a very broad sense. The concept of Bhāṇā has also been widely used in ordinary Punjābī life and culture. This aspect of bhāṇā will be considered in detail a little later. Before that a few remarks are necessary about the meaning of rajā. A brief discussion of hukama has taken place already in Chapter Four (4.1) and in this Chapter (5.4.2.), which will be continued before taking up the examination of bhāṇā.

Rajā as has already been mentioned, is from an Arabic root and means 'pleasure', 'acceptance', 'will', etc.[78] Nānak uses rajā in his hymns with the last meaning, 'will', which is also one of the meanings of bhāṇā.[79] Examples are:

Nānak ekī bēharī hor dūjī nāhī jāi
So kare ji tisai rajāi.[80]

O Nānak, besides the One (Lord), there is no other (living) place.
Whatever He has willed, He does.

In a Vār found in Rāga Mājh Nānak says that he can be called a real Muslim, who accepts the will of His Lord (Raba) and upon whom He shows His mercy. Nānak says:

Raba kī rajāi sir upari karatā manne apu gavāvai.

[77] Kaveeshar Sardul Singh, *Sikh Dharam Darshan* (Panjab), Patiala, 1969 (rpt. 1981), p. 230.
[78] Kahan Singh, p. 1018.
[79] Ibid., p. 913.
[80] *AG*, p. 474.

Tu Nānak sarab jīā miharammati[81] *hoi*
ta Musalamāṇu kahāvai.[82]

He should accept the will of the Lord,
He should accept the Creator above himself.
So O Nānak, may be the Lord who shows His compassion to all, may be (to him) also,
Then he can be called a Muslim.

We can now leave the discussion on rajā in order to begin the examination of bhāṇā. The concept of bhāṇā is important, because it is here that one finds the deepest thought of Nānak. However, scholars seem to have ignored it, because it is difficult to understand both from the linguistic point of view and also from that of usage. For example, Shackle while giving the meaning of the term bhāṇā (pleasure, will, favour), has suggested a possible Sanskrit root, bhāi. According to him, a word used in Nānak's hymns, bhāe or bhāvai, means 'please', 'be pleasing to', 'be acceptable to'. He has put a question mark against his reference to the Sanskrit root of the term bhāṇā.[83] He seems to have been quite right in doubting it, because the famous Sanskrit scholar Monier-Williams gave the meaning of bhāṇā as 'appearance, evidence, perception',[84] which does not at all convey the meaning of Nānak's bhāṇā. But what about Shackle's other suggestion about the Sanskrit root of bhāṇā being bhāi (bhāe, bhāvai)? Concerning this root again no help is found even in the Sanskrit sources. For example, Shackle in his comments on the root bhāi again suggests that it might be connected with the terms bhāti or bhāpayate. But again Monier-Williams gives the menaing of bhati as 'light', 'splendour' or 'evidence' or 'persecution', etc.[85] So these sources, especially those found in Sanskrit are no help in reaching any conclusion about the meaning of bhāṇā in Nānak. But there are a few more sources, particularly in Punjābī, connected both with

[81] Miharammati is another term which Nānak has used. It came into Panjābī from Arabic via Persian, with a root 'mishara' which means 'love', 'compassion', 'favour', etc. (V.S., Kahan Singh, p. 969 and Shackle; p. 240).
[82] *AG*, p. 141.
[83] Shackle, p. 751.
[84] Monier-Williams, p. 751.
[85] Ibid., p. 750.

Sikh religion and with Punjābī usage, which possibly can help in this matter.

As far as the Mahān Kosh of Bhāī Kahan Singh (the Encyclopaedia of Sikh literature) is concerned, it gives three meanings of bhāṇā: (a) the hukama (order) of the Creator, (b) will or desire, and (c) liked.[86] He gives the meaning of bhai, emotion (bhāva), view and thinking,[87] the meaning of bhāv's is similar, except that his list of meanings also includes existence, meaning, birth, soul, nature, world, etc.[88] Bhāī Kahan Singh gives the basic meaning of bhāvai as 'liked' or 'pleased'.[89] He supports his renderings with quotations from the *Ādi Granth.*

The *Panjābī Kosha* gives more detailed meanings of bhāṇā and other related phrases. It also gives a possible evolution of the form of bhāṇā, as follows:

Bhāṇā→Bhāuṇa→Bhāu (Bhāv + ṇa)→Bhāv (Bhāi)

The menaings given in the *Panjābī Kosha* to this term at each stage are also interesting and indicate the development of thought and meaning. Let us start with our key phrase bhāṇā:

i. Bhāṇā: Lord's Order (hukama), will (rajā), desire, fate or destiny, future, will, desire.
The examples of usages are:
Bhāṇā Kartāra da: the Order (hukama) of the Lord.
Bhāṇā Bītanā: the taking place of misfortune (honi)
Bhāṇā Mannaṇa: to accept the will (rajā) of the Lord.
Bhāṇā morana: not allowing misfortune to happen.
Bhāṇā varatau: incident which can take life.
Rabā da Bhāṇā: The will or desire of the Lord.

The *Panjābī Kosha* gives a number of other uses of bhāṇā by people in their daily life.[90]

ii. Bhauṇa: liked, pleased with.[91]

[86] Kahan Singh, p. 913.
[87] Ibid., p. 910.
[88] Ibid., p. 915.
[89] Ibid., p. 916.
[90] *Panjābī Kosha*, vol. IV, p. 544.
[91] Ibid., p. 536.

iii. Bhāu: (Prakrit Bhāv and also Sanskrit Bhāv) respect, profit, love, existence, emotion.[92]

iv. Bhāv: (root Bhā = takes place): emotion, meaning, wish, love, respect, etc.[93]

v. Bhāi: emotion, desire or wish, love, feeling.[94]

From the above data in the *Punjābī Kosha* a number of points become clear. Shackle suggested the possible Sanskrit root, Bhāi, but at the same time expressed his uncertainty, because at the end of his suggestion he put a question mark.[95] There is another point also to be considered about the historical development of the Punjābī language. According to linguistic history, the immediate background of Punjābī is Prakrit not Sanskrit (classical).[96] Therefore the nearest root of bhāṇā, which definitely belongs to the Punjābī language (as we have seen above, there is no such word in Sanskrit), has to be from Prakrit. This root is bhāv (which is also common to Sanskrit); it has another form, Bhā.[97] So it is from Bhā or Bhāv that in the course of time the word bhāṇā came into being in Punjābī, with the comprehensive meanings mentioned above. Bhānā in its connotation as well as usage includes all the meanings of hukama, rajā and even the meaning of nadara, karam, kirapā, diā, etc., because all these follow from His 'Will'.

Bhāṇā represents the total inner (bhāv) of Ik Oṁkār. It was on account of His bhāṇā that he created this world (see Chap. Four, Sec. 4.2.2.1). It is this bhāṇā which can remove all doubts from the inner being of a person. Nānak says:

Jinā bhāṇā kārasu āiā.
Tin Vichu bharamu cukāiā.[98]

Those who have the taste of His Will,

[92] Ibid., p. 556.
[93] Ibid., p. 550.
[94] Ibid., p. 536.
[95] Shackle, p. 225.
[96] Piara Singh Padam, *Punjābī Boli Dā Itihas* (Punjābī), Jullundur, 1969, pp. 52-62.
[97] *Punjābī Kosha*, p. 535.
[98] *AG*, p. 72.

from within them doubts are removed.

His Bhāṇā and He himself are identical. In fact, He acts through His Bhāṇā and controls the whole of human history. His bhāṇā as well as He are absolute and One:

Kiratu paiā naha metai koi
kiā jana kiā āgai hoi.
Jo tisu bhāṇā soī hūā.
Avaru na karaṇai vālādūā.[99]

No one can blot out past actions . . .
What do I know of what will happen hereafter,
Whatever is His will, that only will take place.
Besides Him, no one else is there who does that.

In Rāga Sūhī, Nānak gives a full description of bhāṇā:

Jā tū tā mai sabhu ko tū
Sāhibu merī rāsi jīu.
Tudhu antari hu sukhi vasā
tūṁ antari sābāji jīu.
Bhānāi takhati vadaia
bhāṇāi bhakhi udāsi jīu.
Bhāṇāi thala siri saru
Vahai kamalu phulai ākāsi jīu.
Bhāṇāi bhavajalu langhīai
Bhāṇāi mamajhi bharias jīu.
Bhāṇāi sahu bhīhavālā
hau āvani jāni muīāsi jīu.
Tū sahu agamu atolavā
hu kahi kahi dhahi pāiāsi jīu.
kiā māgau kiā kahi suṇī
mai darasan bhūkh pīāsi jīu.
Gura sabadi sahu pāiā
sacu Nānak ki aradasi jīu.[100]

When I have you, then I have every thing.
Lord, you are my wealth.

[99] *AG*, p. 154.
[100] *AG*, pp. 762-3.

In you, I live in comfort.
Abiding in you, I am honoured.
Through your will one gets the throne and glory.
Through your will one gets consumed and detached.
Through your will the desert is fashioned, the Ocean flows, and in the sky lotuses blossom.
Through your will one crosses the Ocean of this difficult world.
Through your will (the world) is filled.
Through your will you become my joyful Bridegroom, and I get obsessed with the treasury of your good qualities.
Through your will, O my Bridegroom, you become dangerous and I continue to come and go, my hope has become dead.
You, O my Bridegroom, are inaccessible and unweighable.
Calling and calling, finally I fall at your feet.
What should I ask, what should I say and hear, I am hungry and thirsty for your vision.
I have obtained my Bridegroom (Lord) through the Word of my Gurū.
In this way the true prayer of Nānak is heard.

Nānak begins this hymn with full trust in his Sāhịb (Lord). In the part of the hymn about bhāṇā (will) Nānak sees His Lord as having full command of human history. Here too bhāṇā is part of everyday life, just as we saw it expressed through the various pharses and idioms listed in the *Punjābī Kosha.* This hymn at the end once again establishes the Gurū's role, as through him the full vision of the Lord is received. The Lord works in this universe through His bhāṇā.

Now from the above discussion it becomes clear how difficult the concept of bhāṇā is, whereas nadara, kirapā, karam, diā, rajā, hukama are much simpler. The latter also in a real sense only give a limited revelation of the nature of Ik Oṁkār, whereas bhāṇā expresses and reveals His full nature. It does no refer only to compassion, pity, favour, etc., which are parts of (or originate from) His will. Close to the concept of bhāṇā is the concept of parasādi, which we shall examine in the next section.

5.4.3. Parasādi

In the introduction to this chapter it was pointed out that the term parasādi, in conjunction with gura occurs 567 times in the longer or shorter versions of the Mūl Mantr. It also occurs many times together with Gur in the text of Nānak's hymns. A few times it also occurs without gura. For example:

i. . . . *parasādi sukhu pāiā.*[101]

. . . through your parasādi they have received comfort.

ii. *Ihu parasādu gurū te jaṇai.*[102]

This parasadu has been known through the Gurū.

What is the meaning of the term parasādi? A simple translation of this important term has been given by Shackle as "by the favour, grace (of)".[103] Monier-William derived the meaning of parasādi from the root sad, which literally means 'to fall into the power of'. He has also listed various other meanings inferred from its usage in ancient Sanskrit literature. Some of these are; to settle down, to grow clear and bright, to become satisfied or pleased or glad, to be gracious or kind.[104] The meaning of 'sad' has influenced other schemes in their interpretation of parasādi. For example, Bhāī Vir Singh supports his interpretation of parasādi as 'happiness' (parasannatā) and 'mercy' (Kirapālatā) by referring to the same root. He says that when in the mind of a true person, the darkness of tamu (one of three guṇas) and the fear of passion, raju (one of three guṇas) have 'settled down', then the mind of such a person becomes merciful. So according to Bhāī Vīr Singh, the meanings of parasādi are holiness, truthfulness, happiness and mercy.[105]

But again, as in the case of bhāṇā, the *Punjābī Kosha* lists a number of meanings and usages of the term parasādi, which reveal the breadth of its meaning. According to this, parasādi can mean: hapiness, mercy, compassion, an eatable offered to god, food, a special offering of parasāda in the Sikh temple, the left over food of a Gurū, etc. The *Punjābī Kosha* also lists different usages in idiomatic Punjābī.[106]

[101] *AG*, p. 433.
[102] *AG*, p. 1289.
[103] Shackle, p. 181.
[104] Monier-Williams, p. 696.
[105] Vīr Singh, p. 32 (fn).
[106] *Punjābī Kosha*, vol. IV, p. 60.

i. Parasāda Sukhaṇa: to make a commitment for a special offering.

ii. Parasāda Sakanā: to take food.

iii. Parasāda pāṇi: bread and water.

iv. Sita Parasāda: left over food of a Gurū.

v. Karāha Parasāda: a special sweet made out of wheat flour for free distribution in a Sikh Temple.

vi. Pōla Parasāda: Beating with shoes.

vii. Maham Parasādā: Goat meat killed with one stroke.

viii. Parasādā: Food.

ix. Parasādi: Merciful, or one who shows favour.

So the point to be noted here is that when Nānak used the term parasādi, his listeners would have known all these meanings and according to the context they would have understood what he meant. Once again it is not possible to render all these meanings with one term in English.

It is always the context which decides the meaning. In the two hymns quoted at the beginning of this sub-section, it is clear from their context that in each case the meaning of parasādi is 'mercy' or 'favour'.

5.5. GURPARASĀDI

When we come to the instances of parasādi in combination with gura, we find that they have different shades of meanings. There are instances, when they occur as a single phrase, in which parasādi has the same simple meaning, mercy or favour. Examples are:

i. *Gura parasādi aisī mati avai;*
Taṁ kāmaṇi kantai mani bhāvaī.[107]

Through the favour of the Gurū, the bride receives such wisdom, then she becomes pleasing to her husband.

[107] *AG*, p. 357.

ii. *Gura parasādi karam kamāu.*[108]

Through the favour of the Gurū I do good works.

iii. *Gura parasādi param padu pāī.*[109]

Through the favour of the Gurū I obtained the supreme status.

iv. *Gura parasādi range rātā.*[110]

Through the favour of the Gurūi get obsessed with the love (of the Lord).

v. *Gura parasādi ubare sacā nāmu samūli.*[111]

Through the favour of the Gurū one gets saved and meditates on the true Name.

Many more examples can be quoted in which Nānak used parasādi in the sense of 'favour', or 'mercy'. Even kirapā whose meaning is closer to 'compassion' than to 'favour' or 'mercy', is used together with gura in the same sense (favour, mercy) in some hymns of Nānak.[112]

There is, however, a very special use of gurparasādi when it is used in relation to the revelation or knowledge of Ik Oṁkār or Brahamu. In such cases the meaning of parasādi is very close to bhāṇā (see 5.4.2). In these hymns Nānak lays stress on the concept of self-revelation or the self-expression, self-communication or self-manifestation of Ik Oṁkār, since for Nānak, the Gurū is either Ik Oṁkār Himself or His Word (see 5.3.3). There are many hymns in which Nānak used gura parasādi in this sense, and we now quote some of these in support of this argument:

i. *Gura parasādi bhujhi saci samāiā.*[113]

By the grace of the Gurū one discovers and has communion with the Truth.

ii. *Gura parasādi Brahami samāu.*[114]

[108] *AG*, p. 415.
[109] *AG*, p. 838.
[110] *AG*, p. 945.
[111] *AG*, p. 1009.
[112] *AG*, pp. 932, 1027, etc.
[113] *AG*, p. 147.
[114] *AG*, p. 335.

By the grace of the Gurū I have communion with Brahamu.

iii. *Gura parasādi pāiā jāi.*[115]

By the grace of the Gurū one obtained (the Lord).

iv. *Gura parasādi jāṇīai tau anabhu pāvai.*[116]

By the grace of the Gurū one receives wisdom, then one obtains the Fearless (Lord).

v. *Gura parasādi akathu kathīai kahau Kahāai soi.*[117]

By the grace of the Gurū, I describe Indescribable (Lord), and I say what He wants me to say.

vi. *Gura parasādi ghara hī paragāsiai sahaje sahaji samaī.*[118]

By the grace of the Gurū, (the Lord) has become manifest (in my own) home and I have communion with Him.

Here it is important to note that our rendering of parasādi as 'grace' should not be taken as similar to the Christian doctrine of grace; it is best understood as His bhāṇā, will.[119]

5.6. CONCLUDING REMARKS

Gurparasādi, the phrase with which he ends the Mūl Mantr, is the climax of Nānak's basic doctrine of the Ultimate Reality, for which he uses the expression of Ik Oṁkār. Gurparasādi is what makes possible the revelation of Ik Oṁkār, and it is at the same time self-revelation, because He Himself is the Gurū or Sabad (Word), Sabad Gurū (see 5.3.3). Ik Oṁkār is the Gurū of gurūs (human). The basis of his self-revelation is His bhāṇā (will) (see 5.4.2). Nadara (favour), Karama (mercy), Kirapā (compassion), diā (mercy) and rajā (will) (see 5.4.1+2). All these expressions represent different aspects of His bhāṇā; and parasādi (grace) is the sum total of all these expressions. When it is joined with gura as gurparasādi, it becomes the sum total of the nature now revealed as personal (see 5.5) of Ik Oṁkār or Brahamu or the Ultimate Reality.

[115] *AG*, p. 661.
[116] *AG*, p. 725.
[117] *AG*, p. 1033.
[118] *AG*, p. 1273.
[119] Cf. Mcleod, op. cit., p. 206.

CHAPTER SIX

Summary and Conclusion

6.1. SUMMARY

From our study of the content of the hymns of Nānak, it is clear that though these contain all the basic matter for the formation of a systematic theology, yet Nānak himself cannot be brought under the category of a systematic theologian; he was basically a religious person (see Introd. Sec. 2) and was not concerned to provide rational answers to the various questions of human life. The content of his hymns is the outcome of his spiritual experience and his direct encounters with the Ultimate Reality. This is what he himself told one of his disciples, Lālo: "As the Word of the Lord comes to me, the same I let others know" (see Chap. Five, Sec. 5.3.3). Secondly, Nānak's basic concern in life was the human need, which he expressed at the beginning of his most important work, Japu, in the form of a question: "How can one be true, how can the veil of false illusion be torn?" This was the concern with which Nānak was engaged in all his hymns; and it was in the course of dealing with this concern that all his thoughts, including those on Ik Oṁkār or the Ultimate Reality, took form (see Chap. Four, Sec. 4.1). But again this second factor is related to the first one, because Nānak's treatment of any life issue is always based upon his personal religious experiences (see Chap. Five, Sec. 5.3.5).

In Chapter One, the first unit of the Mūl Mantr, the Basic Credal Statement of Sikh religion was examined along with various important related expressions used by Nānak in his hymns. These expressions included ik ekaṁkār (1.3.1), avaru nā dūjā (1.3.2), eka mahi saraba saraba mehi eka (1.3.3), nirālā (1.3.4) and Oṁkār (1.4). The examination of these expressions and the content of the hymns in which they are used, helped to explain the meaning of Nānak's key expression Ik Oṁkār. The repeated use of Ik 'One' and the newly coined expression ekaṁkāru, 'Only One Being', threw further light on the figure '1' which Nānak added before Oṁkār at the beginning of Mūl Mantr. In the same way, avaru nā dūjā, 'there is no second', and nirālā, 'unique', further helped in drawing out the meaning of the figure '1' along with Oṁkār. These expressions were particularly helpful in showing the absolute or ultimate aspect of the nature Oṁkār. The examination of the expression 'eka mahi saraba saraba mehi eka', 'All in One, One in all, added to our understanding of the basis for deep communion, namely, the all-pervasive presence of Oṁkār. But in all the hymns, Nānak's use of various personal titles for his Ik Oṁkār laid stress also on his personal aspect. These titles included dātā (giver), prabhū (Lord), karatā (creator), pātisāhu (king), etc. (see Chap. One, Sec. 1.4.1, and Chap. Two, Sec. 2.4.3). The whole discussion in chapter One led finally to the tentative conclusion that the expressions used by Nānak to open his Basic Credal Statement, 1 Oṁkār means 'One Ultimate Reality' or 'One Absolute Being (see Chap. One, Sec. 1.5).

In Chapter Two, our study showed that Nānak used a variety of names to address his Ik Oṁkār or Param Tattu (the Supreme Reality) or Niraṁkāru (the Formless) (2.4). Nānak used these names (taking into account the context, that is, when addressing people of different religious backgrounds) to make clear to them how he understood the Ultimate Reality and its relationship with human beings. These names reveal the universality of his cardinal doctrine (2.4.3). These different names in no way hamper him in communicating the 'Oneness' or the 'absolute' aspect of his doctrine. On other hand, through the use of these numerous names Nānak highlighted the endless divine (devi) qualities of the Supreme Being (Oṁkāru or Paramesaru) or the Ultimate Reality. But to express the aspect of Ika Oṁkāru as 'Reality' he used the term Sati (2.3.1), and to express the totality of the nature of Sati, he used the term nāmu (2.3.2.). Taken together these two expressions, satināmu, represent the wholeness of Nānak's basic doctrine, or the thought behind Ik Oṁkār (1.5).

In Chapters Three and Four of this work, the various attributes (guṇa) of Ik Oṁkār were investigated. In Chapter Three two aspects of Ik Oṁkār's nature were discussed, nirguṇa (literally, attributeless) and saguṇa (literally with attributes). However, with regard to nirguṇa the main point to be grasped is that it does not in fact mean 'without attributes' and does not mean that Ik Oṁkār has no attributes; it actually refers to those attributes which human beings can only affirm, because they belong only to Ik Oṁkār. On the other hand saguṇa represents those attributes which a human being can experience, or through which a person experiences the personal nature of Ik Oṁkār. Nirguṇa attributes include: oneness, being omnipresent, omnipotent, invisible, infinite, inaccessible, imperceptible, self-existence, etc.; and saguṇa attribute include; bestower, giver, saviour, merciful, gracious, etc. (3.2). In the third Chapter we also examined the basic guṇas of Ik Oṁkār, as listed by Nānak in the Mūl Mantr (3.3). These are: the Creator, personal being, without hostility, temporally eternal, being, above the limitations of human birth and self-born (3.4). The two aspects of Ik Oṁkār, absolute and personal, are again stressed by these basic guṇa. The creator, personal being or eternal being, represents the personal aspect, and the remaining guṇa indicate the absolute aspect of Ik Oṁkār's nature.

In Chapter Four one of the basic guṇa of Ik Oṁkār, Karatā (Creator), was investigated. This investigation showed that all that is seen in this universe is created by the Creator, the Creator being Ika Oṁkāru (4.2). Both the Creator and the creation are real (4.3). Two main conclusions from the whole discussion in Chapter Four are that Ik Oṁkār has revealed or manifested Himself through the creation and that Ik Oṁkār is the sovereign Lord of creation but that the distinction between Him and His created world remains.

Chapters One to Four of this work deal with the nature and attributes of Ik Oṁkār, the 'One Ultimate Reality' or One Absolute Being', based upon Nānak's experiences as found in his hymns. Throughout the present work it has been seen that the nature of Nānak's Ik Oṁkār has two aspects, for one which the term 'absolute' or transcendent was used, and for the other 'personal'. In the hymns which refer to guṇa these are nirguṇa and saguṇa. These two aspects of Ik Oṁkār's nature Nānak established by describing the two sets of attributes—one set which belongs only to Him (oneness, infinity, etc.) and can only be affirmed; and the other known through human experience (giver, saviour, etc.), But how can an ordinary person experience all this? The answer according to Nānak is by the grace of the Gurū (gurparasādi) (5.1.5.2). This is what was discussed in Chapter Five.

Nānak's Ik Oṁkār does not take the form of a human being or any other living being in His saguṇa state (3.2). He is known only through those attributes, which belong to his saguṇa aspect and these can only be experienced through the Gurū's grace (5.3.5). As far as Nānak is concerned this Gurū is Ik Oṁkār Himself, or His Word (5.3.3). But meeting with the Gurū also depends upon His grace (5.3.4). To express the various aspects of grace, Nānak used various words—nadara (favour), Karama (mercy), Kirapā (compassion), diā (mercy), rajā (will) (5.4), which are all aspects of the stronger expression bhāṇā (will) (5.4.2). Parasādi is the sum total of all these expressions, and when it is joined with gur as gurparasādi, it represents the sum total of the revelation of the personal nature (5.5) of Ik Oṁkār (5.6).

6.2. CONCLUSION

In conclusion it can be stated without doubt that Nānak did believe in the Ultimate Reality. The sum total of this Reality is found in his use of the supreme expression 1/Ik Oṁkār, by which he possibly meant the 'One Ultimate Reality' or 'One Absolute Being'.

Throughout his hymns Nānak very clearly lays stress on the two aspects of the nature of 1 Oṁkār: (a) His being absolute and transcendent, which includes His distinction from the things of this universe; and (b) His being personal and immanent, which is chiefly seen through His all-pervading presence in everything in this universe.

Nānak also stressed the numerous attributes under the categories of nirguṇa and saguṇa, which in the case of the first category a human being can only affirm and in the case of the second category, a human being both experiences and affirms. In the case of the second category, the important point according to Nānak is that the Ultimate Reality in which he believed, does not take the form of a human being to reveal itself; instead of that, this revelation comes through its all-pervading presence in the created world.

From Nānak's hymns it is also clear that the relationship between 1 Oṁkār and the visible universe (including human beings) is that between the Karatā (creator) and the creation (Sirathi). As Karatā,

He also takes care of everything in the universe. The stress is thus laid on the personal relationship.

Further Nānak also tells us in his hymns that human beings can know or experience the Ultimate Reality or 1 Oṁkār only through His grace, of which the channel is the Gurū (not the human Gurū as such), or through His 'Word'.

Finally the uniqueness of Nānak's doctrine of the Ultimate Reality can be seen from the way in which he has composed Mūl Mantr—At the beginning he places the figure '1' as a symbol of absoluteness/the ultimate, which is real (sati) in nature; and at the end he places 'parasādi' (grace), the channel by which the '1' can be known, but both the '1' and 'parasādi' are part of the nature of the same Reality the 1/Ik Oṁkār.

Abbreviations

AG: *Ādi Srī Gurū Granth Sāhib Jī*, Srī Damadamī Bīṛ, Panā 1430, Parkāsak Bhāī Javahar Singh Kirpāl Singh and Kampanī, Srī Ammritsar, n.d.

Apte: Apte, Vaman Shivram, *The Practical Sanskrit-English Dictionary*, Delhi, 4th rev. enl. edn. 1965.

Faridakot: *Ādi Srī Gurū Granth Sāhib Jī–Satīka* (Farīdakot Vālā Tīkā), Bhāsā Vibhāg Panjāb, Jilada 1, Patiala, 1970 (rpt).

Gopal Singh: Gopal Singh (trans.): *Srī Gurū Granth Sahib* (English version), 4 vols. Chandigarh, rev. 1978.

GURDĀS: Cakara, Amar Singh (ed.): *Varān Giān Ratanāvalī Bhāī Gurdās Jī*, Shiromani Guraduārā Parbandhak Kametī, Srī Amritsar, 1981.

Kahan Singh: Kahan Singh (Bhāī): *Gurūsabad Ratanākar Mahān Kos* (in Panjābī), Patiala, 1981 (rpt).

Macauliffe: Macauliffe, Max Arthur: *The Sikh Religion, Its Gurūs, Sacred Writings and Authors*, 6 vols., Delhi, 1963 (rpt).

Man Mohan Singh: Man Mohan Singh (trans.): *Srī Gurū Granth Sahib* (English and Panjābī Translation), 8 vols., Amritsar, vol. 1—1962, vols. 2, 3, 5—1964, vol. 4—1964, vols. 7, 8—1969.

Mcleod 1968: Mcleod, W.H.: *Gurū Nānak and the Sikh Religion*, Oxford, 1968.

Mcleod 1975: Mcleod, W.H.: *The Evolution of the Sikh Community*, Delhi, 1975.

Mcleod 1984: Mcleod, W.H.: *Textual Sources for the Study of Sikhism*, Manchester, 1984.

Monier-Williams: Monier-Williams, Sir Monier: *A Sanskrit-English Dictionary*, Oxford, 1989 (rpt).

Punjābī Kosha: Punjābī Kosha, Bhāsā Vibhāga, 6 vols., Patiala, vol. 1—n.d., vol. 2—1970, vol. 3—1967, vol. 4—1971, vol. 5—1982, vol. 6—1983.

Sāhib Singh: Sāhib Singh (Tīkākār): *Ādi Srī Gurū Granth Sāhib Darapaṇ*, Pothī Pahilī, Jalandhar, 1972 (rpt).

Shackle: Shackle, C: *A Gurū Nānak Glossary,* London, 1981.

Talib: Talib, Gurbachan Singh (trans.): *Ādi Srī Gurū Granth Sahib* (in English translation), Patiala, vol. 1—1984, vol. 2—1985, vol. 3—1987 and vol. 4—1990.

Trumpp: Trumpp, Earnest (trans.): *The Ādi Granth* or *The Holy Scripture of the Sikhs,* London, 1977.

Vīr Singh 1971: Bhāī Sāhib Dakatar Vīr Singh Jī (ed.): *Puratan Janam Shākhī—Srī Gurū Nānak Deva Jī,* Amritsar, 1971.

Vīr Singh 1981: Bhāī Sāhib Dakatar Vīr Singh Jī: *Santha Srī Gurū Granth Sāhib Jī, Pothī Pahilī Vichon Japujī Sāhiba,* Amritsar, 1981.

Note: The transcription of Gurumukhi spellings' system is followed in the case of those names or terms, which are originally written in Punjābī with Gurmukhi script. In the case of English, spellings of Punjābī names or terms as used therein are retained throughout this study.

Glossary

Ādi	:	first or primal.
Agamu	:	inaccessible.
Agocaru	:	imperceptible.
Ajonī	:	un-wombed.
Ajūnī	:	not entering existence.
Akāla	:	above the limitations of time.
Akhari	:	through words.
Amaru	:	immortal.
Ārtī	:	performing religious ritual by the use of lighted lamps.
Asaṅkha	:	countless.
Bāṇī	:	Word or Gurū's teaching.
Bhāī	:	Brother or a title used for the outstanding Sikhs of learning and piety.
Bhakta	:	a devotee or exponent of bhakti.
Bhaktī	:	loving devotion.
Bhāsā	:	language.
Bhavaru	:	the soul.
Bīṛ	:	Version
Damadamā	:	resting place.
Dasavāṁ	:	tenth.
Duāru	:	door.
Eku/eka	:	one.
Ekaṁkāru	:	One Absolute Being.
Ghaṭi	:	heart.
Gosaṭi	:	discourse.
Granth	:	Book.
Guṇa	:	attributes or qualities.
Gupatu	:	hidden or unmanifested.
Gurduvārā	:	Sikh temple.
Gurmukha	:	a follower of Gurū.
Gurmukhi	:	script used for writing Punjābī language.

Gurū/Gur	:	Teacher or a spiritual preceptor.
Gyānī	:	a sikh scholar or theologian.
Hukamu	:	command or order.
Ik	:	one.
Janama	:	birth.
Japu	:	recitation.
Jatī	:	caste or kind.
Jī	:	a honorific suffix.
Jīlad	:	volume.
Joṛ	:	spelling.
Jotī	:	light.
Karama	:	deeds or actions.
Karamu	:	favour or mercy.
Karatā	:	maker or Creator.
Kāru	:	only.
Kosa	:	dictionary.
Khālsā	:	the Sikh brotherhood instituted by the tenth Gurū Gobind Singh.
Khāri	:	bitter.
Khatrī	:	a mercantile caste.
Mahalā	:	a term used in the *Ādi Granth* to distinguish works of different Gurūs.
Mahāna	:	big or large.
Māyā	:	illusion.
Mūl	:	root or basic.
Mundana	:	a name of ritual involving the shaving of a head as a child.
Mantr	:	a verse or word or syllable of particular religious importance.
Mūrati	:	being or form.
Nāmu	:	Name
Nātha	:	master, a yoga sect well known at the time of Nānak.
Nirabhaü	:	without fear.
Nirguṇa	:	without attributes.
Nirālā	:	unique.
Nirālāmu	:	disassociated.
Niramalu	:	pure of holy.

Niraṁkarū	:	the Formless One.
Nirañjanu	:	absolutely pure.
Niravairu	:	without hostility.
Oṁkār	:	One Absolute Being or One Ultimate Reality.
Pahilī	:	first.
Paragatu	:	revealed or manifest.
Parama	:	supreme.
Parasādu	:	grace or favour.
Parbhū	:	the Lord.
Pātisāhu	:	king.
Paüṛi	:	stanza.
Pothī	:	volume.
Purukhu	:	man or the personal Being.
Paṇḍit	:	learned (Brahman).
Qāzi	:	Muslim judge or scholar.
Rāgu	:	musical mode or music.
Rekha	:	line or outline.
Rūpu	:	form or appearance.
Sacā	:	true, real.
Sāhibu	:	Lord.
Saiṁbhaü	:	self-born.
Sākhī	:	testamony or story.
Saloka	:	couplet or verse or stanza.
Saṁmata	:	an Indian name of year which is known as Bikarami year, which was started 57 years before Christ.
Sant	:	synonym for Sādhu, which means an ascetic.
Santhā	:	lesson or reading.
Saraba	:	all.
Sati	:	truth or reality.
Sātīk	:	commentary.
Sikh	:	discipline.
Singh	:	lion.
Saguṇa	:	with attributes.
Sodar	:	a name of selection of hymns from the *Ādi Granth*, used at the early evening as a Sikh prayer.
Soḍhi	:	a subcaste of second varna (caste), i.e.

		Kshatriya (the warrior caste) to which last seven Gurūs belonged.
Sohilā	:	hymn of joy.
Sūfī	:	a Muslim mystic.
Savaīe	:	penegyric, praise song.
Tantu	:	essence.
Tīkā	:	Interpretation.
Tīkākārā	:	Interpreter.
Tribhavaṇu	:	the three worlds.
Vār	:	ballad, song of praise, eulogy, etc., plural of Vāra is Varān.
Vaiṣṇara	:	the sect, which worship the god Vishnu.
Vibhāg	:	department.
Vichon	:	from.
Wahigurū	:	Wonderful Lord or Teacher.
Yogī	:	One who practices yoga is called a Yogi. Yoga is a method leading to a state of liberation through the union of the human spirit with the Ultimate Reality.

Bibliography

A. PRIMARY WORKS

a. Original Texts in Punjābī

Ādi Srī Gurū Granth Sāhib Jī, Srī Damadamī Bīṛ, Panā 1430, Parkāsak Bhāī Javahar Singh Kirpāl Singh and Kampanī, Srī Ammritsar, n.d.

Cākar, Amar Singh (ed.): *Varān Giān Ratanāvalī Bhāī Gurdas Jī,* Shiromanī Gurduārā Parbandhak Kametī, Srī Ammritsar, 1981.

Kirpāl Singh (ed.): *Janama Sākhī Srī Gurū Nānak Deva Jī,* Likhata Srī Meharabāns Jī Soḍhi, Amritsar, vol. 1, 1962.

Janam Sākhī Srī Gurū Nānak Dev Jī, Pothi Harijī te Pothī Caturabhuj, Amritsar, vol. II, 1969.

Kirapāl Singh (ed.): *Bhāī Manī Singh Vālī Janam Sākhī,* Janam Sākhī Paramparā by Kirapāl Singh, Patiala, 1969, pp. 330-401.

Kohalī, Surindar Singh (ed.): *Janama Sākhī Bhāī Bālā,* Chandigarh, 1975.

Piāra Singh (ed.): *Sanbhū Nāth Vālī Janam Patrī Bābe Nānak Jī Kī— Parsidh Nān Ādi Sakhīān,* Jalandhar, 1969.

Bhāī Sāhib Dakatar Vīr Singh Jī (ed.): *Purātan Janam Sākhī—Srī Gurū Nānak Dev Jī,* Amritsar, 1971 (7th edn.).

b. Commentaries and Translations of the *Ādi Granth* and Japu

I. *Punjabī*

Ādi Srī Gurū Granth Sāhib Jī—Sātīka (Farīdakot Vālā Tīkā), Bhāsā Vibhāg Punjāb, Jilad 1, Patiala, 1970 (rpt).

Jodh Singh (Bhāī): Japuji Satīk, Patiala, 1980.

Sāhib Singh (Tīkākār): *Srī Gurū Granth Sāhib Darapaṇ,* Pothī Pahilī, Jàlandhar, 1972 (rpt).

Bhāī Sāhib Dakatar Bhāī Vīr Singh JĪ: *Santhā Srī Gurū Granth Sāhib Jī,* Pothī Pahilī Vichon Japujī Sāhib, Amritsar, 1981.

II. *Hindi*

Vinoba: *Japuji* (*Mūl Ke Sath*), Varanasi, April 1965.

III. *German*

Thiel-Horstmann, Monika, Mūlamantra, Japuji, Leben Aus Der Wahrheit Zürich, 1988, pp. 35-59.

IV. *English*

1. COMPLETE TEXT OF THE *ĀDI GRANTH*

Gopal Singh (trans.): Srī Gurū Granth Sahib (English version), 4 vols., Chandigarh, rev. 1978.

Man Mohan Singh (trans.): *Srī Gurū Granth Sahib* (English and Punjābī translation), 8 vols., Amritsar, vol. 1—1962, vols. 2, 3, 5—1964, vols. 4, 6—1964, vols. 7, 8—1969.

Talib, Gurbachan (trans.): *Srī Gurū Granth Sahib* (in English translation), 4 vols., Patiala, vol. 1—1984, vol. 2—1985, vol. 3—1987 and vol. 4–1990.

2. PARTIAL TEXT OF THE *ĀDI GRANTH*

Macauliffe, Max Arthur: *The Sikh Religion Its Gurūs*, Sacred Writings and Authors, 6 vols., Oxford, 1909.

Trumpp, Earnest (trans.): *The Ādi Granth or The Holy Scripture of the Sikhs*, London, 1877.

3. TEXT OF *JAPU*

Dewan Singh: *Gurū Nānak's Message in Japujī*, Amritsar, 1970, pp. 81-119.

Doabia, Harbans Singh: *Sacred Nit-Nem*, Amritsar, 1985, pp. 1-57.

Mcleod, W.H.: Textual Sources for the Study of Sikhism, Manchester, 1984 pp. 86-93.

Puran Singh: *Japjī Sahib, Gurū Nānak and His Japjī* by Parkash Singh, Amritsar, 1969, pp. 64-85.

Sohan Singh: *The Seeker's Path* (Being an Interpretation Gurū Nānak's Japujī), Bombay, 1959.

Teja Singh: *The Japjī*, Ammritsar, 1974 (7th edn.).

B. REFERENCES/WORKS

1. PUNJĀBĪ

Harakīrat Singh (ed.): *Pānjabī Sabad*—Jor Kos, vol. 4, Patiala, 1983.

Kahan Singh (Bhāī): *Gurūsabad Ratanākar Mahān Kos*, Patiala, 1981 (rpt).

Pānjabī Kos, Bhāsā Vibhāg, 6 vols., Patiala, vol. 1—n.d., vol. 2—1970, vol. 3—1967, vol. 4—1971, vol. 5—1982, vol. 6—1983.

2. Punjābī-English

Shackle, C.: *A Gurū Nānak Glossary*, London, 1981.

3. English-Punjābī

Teja Singh: *Anglo-Punjabī Dictionary*, Ludhiana, 1964 (2nd edn.).

4. Sanskrit-English

Apte, Vaman Shivram: *The Practical Sanskrit-English Dictionary*, Delhi, 4th rev, enl. edn. 1965.

Monier-Williams, Sir Monier: *A Sanskrit-English Dictionary*, Delhi, 1988 (rpt).

C. OTHER WORKS

1. Punjābī

Darada Hir Singh (ed.): *Karam Singh Historian Dī Itihāssak Khoj*, Amritsar, 1975.

Jodh Singh (ed.): *Gurū Nānak Bānī*, Delhi, n.d.

Kavīsar, Saradūl Singh: *Sikha Daram Darasan*, Patiala, 1981.

Padam, Piārā Singh: *Punjābī Bolī Dā Itihāsa*, Jalandhar, 1969.

Prem Parkās Singh: *Gura Nānak Ate Niraguṇa Dhārā*, Patiala, 1973.

Salūjā, Jagajīta Singha: *Mūl Mantar*, Ludhiana, 1982.

2. English

Banerjee, Anil Chandra: *Gurū Nānak and His Times*, Patiala, 1984.

Bhattacharyya, Haridas (ed.): *The Cultural Heritage of India*, vol. IV, Calcutta, 1983 (rpt).

Cole, W. Owen: *The Gurū in Sikhism*, London, 1982.

Cole, W. Owen and Piara Singh Sambhi: *The Sikhs, Their Religious Beliefs and Practices*, Delhi, 1978.

O'Connell, Joseph T. et al. (eds.): *Sikh History and Religion in the Twentieth Century*, Toronto, 1988.

Das, Sunil Kumar: *Srī Caitanya and Gurū Nānak*, Calcutta, 1985.

Dasgupta, Surendra Nath: *A History of Indian Philosophy*, vol. 1, Delhi, 1988 (rpt).

Farquhar, J.N.: *A Primer of Hinduism*, London, 1911.

Ganda Singh (ed.): *The Panjab Past and Present—Sources of the Life and Teachings of Gurū Nānak*, vol. III, Patiala, 1969.

Grewal, J.S.: *Gurū Nānak in History*, Chandigarh, 1979 (rpt).

Hymns of Gurū Nānak, Language Department, Patiala, 1972.

Iqbal Singh (Gurū): *Philosophy of Gurū Nānak*, Jodhpur, 1981.

Iyengar, K.R. Srīnivasa (ed.): *Gurū Nānak—A Homage*, Delhi, 1973.
Jacob, Colonel G.A.: *Concordance (Upanishads and Bhagavad Gita)*, Delhi, 1981 (rpt).
Juergensmeyer, Mark and N. Gerald Barrier (ed.): *Sikh Studies—Comparative Perspective on a Changing Tradition*, Berkeley, 1979.
Jones, L. Bevan: *The People of the Mosque*, Delhi, rev. edn. 1980.
Khushwant Singh: *A History of the Sikhs*, vol. 1: *1469-1839*, Bombay, 1986 (rpt).
Kohli Surindar Singh : *A Critical Study of Ādi Granth*, Delhi 1976 (rpt).
——— : *Philosophy of Gurū Nānak*, Chandigarh, 1980 (rpt).
Loehlin, C.H.: *The Granth of Gurū Gobind Singh and The Khalsa Brotherhood*, Lucknow, 1971.
——— : *The Sikhs and Their Scriptures*, Lucknow, 1964.
Macauliffe, Max A.: *The Life and Teaching of Gurū Nānak*, Chandigarh, 1980 (rpt).
Mcleod, W.H.: *Early Sikh Tradition—A Study of Janam Sākhīs*, Oxford, 1980.
——— : *The Evolution of the Sikh Community—Five Eassys*, Oxford, 1975.
——— : *Gurū Nānak and the Sikh Religion*, Oxford, 1968.
Mcmullen, Clarence Osmond: *Religious Beliefs and Practices of the Sikhs in Rural Panjab*, Delhi, 1989.
Phillips, Maurice: *The Teaching of the Vedas*, Delhi, 1976 (rpt).
Pickthall, Mohammed Marmadake (trans.): *The Meaning of the Glorious Koran*, Delhi, 1988 (rpt).
Pritam Singh (ed.): *Sikh Concept of the Divine*, Amritsar, 1985.
Radhakrishnan, S.: Indian Philosophy, vol. 1, London, 1951 (rpt).
Sahib Kaur: *Sikh Thought*, Delhi, n.d.
Sarma, D.S.: *Hinduism Through the Ages*, Bombay, 1961.
Schomer, Karine and W.H. Mcleod (eds.): *The Saints—Studies in a Devotional Tradition of India*, Delhi, 1987.
Sher Singh: *Philosophy of Sikhism*, Amritsar, 1986 (rpt).
Smart, Ninian: *Doctrine and Argument in Indian Philosophy*, London, 1964.
Sutantar Singh: *About Siri Guru Granth Sahib*, Delhi, 1976.
Talib, Gurbachan Singh: *Guru Nanak, His Personality and Vision*, Delhi, 1969.
Trilochan Singh: *Guru Nanak, Founder of Sikhism (A Biography)*, Delhi, 1969.

D. JOURNALS

Journal of Sikh Studies, vol. VI, no. 2, August 1979, Department of Guru Nanak Studies, Guru Nanak Dev University, Amritsar.

Religion and Society, vol. XI, no. 1, March 1964, Bulletin of the Christian Institute for the Study of Religion and Society, Bangalore.

Studies in Sikhism and Comparative Religion, vol. VI, no. 2, October 1987, Guru Nanak Foundation, Delhi.

Studies in Sikhism and Comparative Religion, vols. VII, no. 1 and 2, April-October 1988, Guru Nanak Foundation, Delhi.

Vidyajyoti : Journal of Theological Reflection, vol. 45, May 1981, The Vidyajoyti Educational and Welfare Society (Views), Delhi.

Index